smart
dating

About Mary Balfour

Following a successful career which included photography, modelling, community work and running an inner-city adult education centre, Mary Balfour bought her first introduction agency, *Drawing Down the Moon*, in 1986. This was *the* original personal introduction agency in the UK and now caters for well-educated professionals.

Her mission in life is to help people find the love they seek and have fun in the process. Over the years she has studied the behaviour patterns of people who are successful in finding a partner and she believes that these can be analysed and learned. To this end she has developed the concept of 'Domino Dating', her strategy for creating high-calibre dating opportunities, which has triggered many happy endings.

Mary also enjoys:

♡ **Running 'Singles' Seminars' on the art of successful dating.**

♡ **Date coaching on a one-to-one basis.**

♡ **Public-speaking engagements on any aspect of her work.**

Known as the UK's matchmaking guru, Mary is a seasoned media commentator and has appeared in numerous television and radio programmes. She has also featured in many magazine and newspaper articles.

Mary lives with her husband Sebastian, a professor at the London School of Economics, in Kensington, London. She has two stepdaughters, Rosa and Marianna.

FREE DATING MEMBERSHIP!

Readers of Smart Dating get one month's FREE full membership of Mary's internet dating sites. Just visit www.SmartDating.co.uk for smart people everywhere or www.GrownUpDating.co.uk where attractive older singles meet. When prompted enter the promotion code "Smart Dating".

smart dating

how to find your man

mary balfour

Mary Balfour Publications London
www.drawingdownthemoon.co.uk

Second edition published 2008 by Mary Balfour Publications

Information: www.drawingdownthemoon.co.uk

First edition published 2004 by Element
An Imprint of HarperCollins*Publishers*
77–85 Fulham Palace Road
Hammersmith, London W6 8JB

Text illustrations by Nick Roberts

A catalogue record for this book is
available from the British Library

ISBN 978-0-9560760-0-7

Contents

Acknowledgements

A number of people have contributed to the writing of this book with ideas, personal accounts and moral support.

First, I have to say how profoundly grateful I am to all the members of my introduction agency, Drawing Down the Moon (and also Only Lunch and Love and Friends, which I no longer own). Many have shared with me their deepest feelings and secrets about their search for a loving partner and without them this book would not have been possible. Naturally their identities have been changed for reasons of confidentiality.

My past and present staff and consultants, of whom I am so proud, deserve much more than heartfelt thanks for everything they have done to bring about so many happy endings. They feel as passionately as I do about the value of passing on the strategies for success and failure in the dating game. Cath, Debi, Edwina, Frances, Georgie, Georgina, Harjit, Kate, Sophie , Sally, Sam and more recently, Terry and Lizzie – your care of Agency members, your feedback and humour have been wonderful.

Miia Koponen is the owner of the sunny voice that so often greets our Agency callers. She is also an inspired and hardworking matchmaker to whom many people owe their happiness. Well done, Miia.

Caroline Frost has done much matchmaking and interviewing in Drawing Down the Moon in the past and now concentrates on headhunting suitable matches for us from further afield. Caroline, you are a woman with a mission – I know I can rely upon you to track down that elusive and special individual who ticks many boxes on some expectant member's wish list.

Jane Parsons, my Office Manager, became a crucial part of my life and the life of the agencies whilst I was writing this book in its first edition. Jane, your loyalty, professionalism, hard work and dedication to the cause are admirable. I feel not only affection, but also gratitude to you for freeing me up and enabling Smart Dating to happen.

Kate Kennedy, my Senior Matchmaker, who is also a trained psychotherapist, has amazed many clients by encouraging them to overcome negative attraction patterns and as a result, blossom and meet their future sweethearts. Your seventeen years making magic at Drawing Down the Moon, Kate, have been a major part of our achievement.

I owe much inspiration for this second edition of Smart Dating to Pier Reid, who is the General Manager of Drawing Down the Moon with special responsibility for business development. The imagination you have displayed in developing strategies for "headhunting" outside and inside the Agency and also for stream-lining the office administration has enabled us to reach new levels of success. Pier, your drive and humour, together with your support for me personally, have been especially appreciated.

Many couples owe their happiness to the multi-talented wizardry of Andy Maccabe Andy who is the MD of the internet dating site, www.LoveandFriends.com. Andy and I were co-founders of this niche site and it is only recently that I have relinquished my share entirely to his excellent stewardship. Andy is also the brains behind www.SmartDating.co.uk and www.GrownUpDating.co.uk. Andy, how brave you were to be the first male to join our coven of females. I am constantly inspired by your imagination and ability to get computers to make love.

Visitors to our website, www.drawingdownthemoon.co.uk may have viewed the videos of Sammy and Tom Murray Brown who met and married through us (Kate Kennedy waved the magic wand) and then so very generously opted to go public to inspire others to take charge of their dating options and make love happen. I am most grateful to you both for this. Sammy has recently given birth to twin boys, Arthur and George. As with the thousands of other (more anonymous) clients who've met their match through Moon endeavours, I wish you both much happiness and many golden years together.

To Julia McCutcheon, my original literary consultant, many thanks for your faith, enthusiasm and for so rapidly finding me my first publishers. Your support during the writing of the first edition was invaluable and much appreciated.

Ann Lloyd, general editor for the first edition, burnt much midnight oil performing the Herculean task of sorting out my disparate ideas and giving them cohesion and meaning. Ann, you have been much more than an editor, you have taught me lots and become a good friend.

I am indebted to Paul McKenna, Michael Breen and Richard Bandler for showing me how NLP techniques can play such a vital part in helping people to create positive dating states.

I am most grateful to Wanda Whiteley, Belinda Budge, Susanna Abbott and all those at ThorsonsElement who believed that the first eddition of Smart Dating published by them would be such a success.

This book would be incomplete without Nick Roberts' wacky cartoons. Thanks, Nick, they're great.

Friends who have contributed ideas and encouragement are too many to name. You know who you are. Please accept my deepest thanks.

My sister Dee Harkin and her family are a staple part of my life – bless you all for your love and encouragement. Dee has joined me to work with the agencies and has contributed much in terms of ideas for client care and promoted new ideas to improve our service.

And, last but not least, Sebastian, my amazing, loving husband and light of my life, thank you for just being you and being there for me throughout the lengthy and often bumpy process of building Drawing Down the Moon and writing my first book. Your suggestions about the many drafts of Smart Dating thrust in front of you have been invaluable. Every day starts with a golden glow just knowing you are next to me.

Introduction

Why this book had to be written and what it's about

I have always enjoyed interfering with other people's lives. First, it was getting my friends fixed up with flats, jobs, kittens and dates. Then it was setting up courses for educationally deprived adults in a run down inner city neighbourhood.

In 1986, I thought it was time to move on so I bought an introduction agency called **Drawing Down the Moon**. I hardly paused for thought. I knew it was exactly what I wanted to do. I had a vision of languishing in a sort of *fin de siècle* salon sipping delicious coffee with fascinating people telling me all about their lives and loves. Of course, I would be able to add that finishing touch they all yearned for by introducing them to their equally fascinating other half.

The dream turned out to be the reality for about 30% of the time. The other 70% was an extraordinary mixture of rapid learning about what makes people fall in and out of love, fending off those I couldn't help and lurching between financial famine and feast.

The learning curve was both enjoyable and intense. I became obsessed with the urge to find out more and I gained a huge amount from studying the approaches that worked and comparing them with those that didn't. I saw thousands of individuals succeed in the love stakes and noted certain formulae emerging as the winners. I also discovered that I could spot the recipes for failure a mile off. So much so that at the three agencies I now run, my staff and I can often predict within a couple of minutes who will get into a good relationship quickly. The others, who will have to learn new strategies first, we call the 'blossomers'.

From years of experience, we know what guidance to give people and what advice is the most constructive. My mission in this book is to share this with women everywhere and help them find the partner they seek – without wasting precious time. I explain how to create and make the most of dating opportunities and take control of one's chances of love in spite of the apparent dearth of commitment-minded men and the chances to meet them in society today. Here's an outline of how it's done.

The Drawing Down the Moon dating success programme

The book comprises a comprehensive 'find your man now' programme tested in 'laboratory conditions' by all the thousands of wonderful men and women we've successfully matched up in my introduction agencies over the last 23 years. It is not written primarily for the lonely singleton but more for the truly fulfilled woman in her own right with lots to offer to a potential partner. I explain how you can create heaps of practical dating opportunities, starting today. This way you can compress a lifetime's worth of dates into just a few months and start **Domino Dating**, the term I've given to my time-tested, dating-for-results strategy.

But what is the point of going on lots of dates if you're scaring men off by giving out go-away signals because you're not in mental or physical 'dating mode'? To this end, there are about 40 **Mansearch Workouts** and **Checklists** designed to wise you up on your individual dating strengths and zap anything likely to sabotage your chances.

Are you having trouble breaking the ice on first dates or following them through into second dates? Well, you'll find here all the practical dating do's and don'ts you'll ever need, culled from member feedback in my introduction agencies. If you've ever had difficulty attracting someone you really fancy then Chapter 8, 'Turn Men On and Pull Them In', is for you. We are all born great flirts and I'll suggest ways you can reclaim your flirt skills to create sexually charged electricity as well as offering time-tested hot tips for saucy seduction.

If you always fancy men who don't fancy you then I explain how you can inoculate yourself against a repeat performance and give you the low-down on how to feel attracted to 'Relationship-Man' rather than 'Rat-Man'.

Smart Dating is liberally sprinkled throughout with '**Lovebytes**' – wise or witty quotes from famous people on the theme of love. My years of matchmaking have provided heaps of illuminating '**Smart Biogs**' to illustrate the value of the suggested Mansearch strategies – all with identities changed, of course.

At the end of each chapter you'll find '**Keynotes & Diary Prompts**' to nudge you into the here and now. Also there are '**Relationship Action Plans**' to keep you goal oriented and, last but not least, suggested '**Treats**' to keep your self-esteem in tip top condition. Lastly, I have included a short **Further Reading** section containing books that I can recommend about many of the topics raised in *Smart Dating*.

Finally, I want to say that although this book is targeted at women and penned from a female perspective, I really appreciate the fact that many curious males have enjoyed reading it as well. If I have caused any offence by passing over a more masculine point of view, I apologize unreservedly.

Happy dating!

Mary

Mary Balfour – MD, Drawing Down the Moon Introduction Agency
www.DrawingDowntheMoon.co.uk   www.SmartDating.co.uk   www.GrownUpDating.co.uk

Fiona was wondering about what they'd call their first child. Mike was ruminating on whether she'd ask him back to her place.

chapter 1

Single Again?

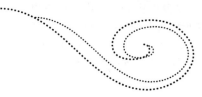

Man-less or positively single?

Let's go straight to the heart of the matter: you're single, smart and independent and, at last, that's cool according to the glossy magazines. Why, then, do so many of you have bookshelves that are stuffed with Guides, Rules and 12-Step Plans for 'Finding and Keeping a Man'?

From among the ranks of those of you who still secretly want a male lover, or a partner or a husband come the inevitable mutterings: 'Why are other women more successful in finding a man than I am?', 'What prevents me from getting there too?', and 'What can I do about it?' You are, after all, very successful, but through a combination of circumstance, bad luck and playing your cards wrong, you keep missing out on the chance of that beautiful relationship.

Take a deep breath – and relax. You're not alone. Everyone knows someone in this situation, and many have been there. It is the epidemic of the new century.

L♡vebyte

" When you really want love, you will find it waiting for you. **"**
Oscar Wilde

My credentials

From the slightly unusual position of someone who has run three different introduction agencies, I've learnt many positive dating strategies that are both practical and psychological. They are strategies that can change your life. Indeed, my observations on the habits of women who've been successful in their partner search fill three bulging filing cabinets! I want to share all this with you.

My privileged position has also clearly shown me the 'blockers' for those who fail to find their man. I've discovered how almost anyone, bar those with deep psychological problems, can overcome these blockers – anyone, that is, who's prepared to explore and experiment creatively with the ideas suggested in the chapters that follow.

Start challenging your relationship blockers right now. Take out your pen and get ready to tackle the practical step-by-step **Mansearch Checklists** and **Workouts** on these pages. Don't hesitate to underline or tick anything that rings a bell for you. This will be an affirmation of your intention to make things happen and it will really help to motivate you.

Above all, this is a book for dipping into to identify tailor-made solutions to your particular relationship blockers and to enhance your innate attractiveness.

Zap the negatives

'But,' you ask, 'aren't there some things you just can't change? If there's a "rat-man" at the party – it's him I make the beeline for! "Decent" men are so boring'. Another common wail is, 'The men I go for are always "married", or "commitment-phobes" or "living on the other side of the world". I'm a bad chooser!' Yes, of course your emotional programming influences everything, especially your patterns of attraction – but it's not set in stone.

L♡vebyte

❝ Faint heart never won fair lay. ❞
Sarah Harrison (English writer)

Working through *Smart Dating*, you will become more aware of your relationship sabotage points. By doing this you can then start to learn what you need to do. After putting into practice the strategies that I suggest, you will find it becomes easier to explore outside your current comfort zone. This way you will become at ease with new and more positive relationship strategies which you might be unconsciously avoiding right now. So, if either 'Rat-Man' or 'Commitment-Phobe' is your particular penchant at present, you can develop attraction for 'Relationship-Man' as well. You don't believe me? Well, it may not happen overnight, but happen it can. I've witnessed it many times.

Tools for the task

Continuing with a positive theme, do you remember a really successful relationship or a successful moment in a relationship? What were the ingredients? Can you pinpoint anything about the strategies that led to it? Can you recreate your state of mind and your emotions?

The idea is to fine-tune your dating techniques and strategies by learning from your own and other people's successes and failures. This is a theme I will continually revisit in *Smart Dating* and it is the key to a happy outcome. One effective technique is to borrow a few tools from **NLP (Neuro-Linguistic Programming)** and **Assertiveness Training**. 'Help!', I can hear some of you say – but don't let the rather fierce terminology deter you! Both these approaches to modifying behaviour offer a user-friendly range of simple techniques. Even the most hard-bitten cynic will find them invaluable in this minefield of finding and building a new relationship.

NLP

Nuero Linguistic Programming defines itself as the study of human excellence. It provides powerful techniques for understanding your own patterns of behaviour and communication in practical terms. It is employed in management, sales, stress relief, phobia treatment, life coaching and in all other aspects of personal development. It can be used to help prepare you to put your best self forward at a job interview, as well as for getting yourself into 'flirt mode' before launching yourself on a terrifying party full of single men whom your best friend says you simply must meet! NLP is not just a theoretical approach, but one based on what has actually worked for others – and for you, too, in your own past.

There is much one can say about NLP but this is not the place. I will simply draw on some of its techniques as one of the resources which you will find particularly helpful in this business of dating. I concentrate on the 'anchoring' and 'triggering' of useful responses, the idea being to try to imagine and then experience the same thoughts, feelings, visions and sounds you had when things were going really well – perhaps when you felt confident and relaxed on a date or with friends. When you've well and truly conjured up the elements of this happy, successful scenario in terms of what you thought, felt, heard and saw, you then 'anchor' these images to a physical 'trigger', such as pressing your thumb and middle finger together. The idea is to use this thumb/finger action as a prompt to invoke the same success-linked thoughts, feelings, sounds and visions on future occasions – such as when you're about to date Mr Wonderful. The result is that you can imagine what a successful outcome would feel, sound and look like. This approach can be used in many situations, but you'll find it particularly useful around dating and attractiveness issues. (*See* Chapter 8, 'Turning Men On and Pulling Them In' for more on NLP techniques for smart flirts).

Assertiveness Training

Assertiveness Training? No, it's not about being bossy and getting your own way – after all what could this possibly have to do with dating? It's about being in touch with your own needs and feelings as well as those of other people. This leads on to communicating effectively with both sensitivity and respect and this is invaluable for negotiating almost any day-to-day relationship problems with flair and success. The philosophy underlying Assertiveness Training is invaluable in a dating situation and indispensable for nipping problems in the bud once you think you've found your man. I will use **Smart Biogs** (histories from the Agency archives) to show how Assertiveness can be used to navigate a smoother path in a bumpy relationship.

I used to teach Assertiveness when I worked in adult education and found that it could change the course of people's lives. It certainly helped to change mine and, in turn, has inspired me to encourage many others to be proactive and successful in their search for someone to love. The stories which follow later in this chapter are about some of these people. I have learned a lot from them and you can too.

New directions

Through my job as a matchmaker I've met all sorts of women. Among those I recall with particular affection are: the manager of a chain of high street shops, a pop icon (sorry, no clues as to who!), a teacher of deaf children, a kitchen-design consultant, a sales co-ordinator (who secretly wanted to do stand-up comedy), a bereavement counsellor, a midwife, a marketing guru, a dot-com millionairess and even a widow whose 14-year-old daughter had phoned us on her behalf. This veritable cocktail of women had one thing in common – they were all looking for someone with whom they could share their lives. Every one of them found that special person, but not without a little nudge in the right direction.

Before they first came to see me, none of these women had a cat in hell's chance of being in a relationship. Why not? Some simply had no chances of meeting available single men. Others were bad choosers or were going about dating in all the wrong ways. Unless they learned from their past, they were likely to repeat these unsuccessful tactics. And learn they did through their experience of dating in the agency. You can do the same – see if any of their remarks about previous relationships apply to you. Have a go at this Mansearch Checklist.

Mansearch Checklist – Nailing the failures

My last relationship finished because ...

	Check
He bolted for the hills when the 'C' word – commitment – was mentioned.	☐
He was the opposite of me in every way.	☐
He said 'No' to marriage because he needed his space.	☐
I fell in love right at the start – too soon; he wasn't ready.	☐
We worked and played too hard – our relationship just fizzled out.	☐
We disliked each other's friends.	☐
He was emotionally damaged.	☐
He said I was suffocating him.	☐
I was terrified of rejection.	☐
I wanted children – he didn't.	☐
Other reasons:	☐

....

These were happy, well-adjusted women who had a great social life and interesting jobs. Why couldn't they handle their love life in an equally effective way? As we talked, the clues – and the keys – to their relationship issues revealed themselves. Here are some of the explanations they'd offer during their initial interview. Have you ever felt the same?

Mansearch Checklist – Learning from the past

I don't find relationships easily because ...

Check

I'm probably too idealistic about what I want.	☐
I find men who are a challenge really exciting.	☐
Men feel threatened by my success in life.	☐
Maybe I rush things.	☐
I'm not meeting attractive, available men because of lack of opportunity and time.	☐
I've a hunch that I unconsciously sabotage potential relationships through simply handling them the wrong way.	☐
Other reasons:	☐

....

Ready to experiment?

After discussions and guidance about strategies, all these women tried at least one aspect of the material covered in my various Workouts. For example, they took more emotional risks, experimented by meeting people in new ways or tried new responses to situations. They started to handle first dates differently. They began to communicate better and to tune into undiscovered dimensions of their personalities. As a result, many of them experienced a surge of self-confidence and self-worth. Make time to reflect on the questions in the Workouts and you too can embark on the same adventure.

S⊙undbyte

Workouts work! How do I know? Because I've seen hundreds of women change the way they seek out a relationship through using key questions, advice and prompts that my colleagues and I have developed and used at my agencies over the years. These have been systematized and incorporated into the Workouts so that you can kick-start some action towards finding and building your new relationship.

Domino Dating

Eliminating one stumbling block will have a knock-on effect and eliminate another. For example, lack of opportunity to meet people can make you doubt yourself psychologically. Your confidence plummets, if only for a while. You feel that there is something wrong with you, rather than with the crazy situation you're in. However, self-esteem is rekindled once you start to enjoy dating regularly again. You are creating opportunities to meet interesting men, and the more you meet the easier it gets. One dating success triggers another – what I call the **Domino Dating Effect**. In other words, go for volume. The more practice you have at dating, the easier it gets to negotiate all the hurdles and recognize and attract men with real relationship potential. Women who practise my Domino Dating strategy seem to be able to find and stay in relationships more easily. Whereas, if you only go on one date a year – even if that date was the cat's whiskers – you are likely to have such high expectations that it fails to take off.

I believe that you can challenge any aspect of the way you organize yourself and your behaviour in relationships, and this will greatly increase the likelihood of success next time round. First, however, you need to clarify your goals.

Ready to relate?

Are you sure you really want a relationship? Perhaps you're actually quite content with being single but have difficulty admitting it. Lots of people give in to social pressures to find a partner when it may be the wrong time for them or simply not what they fundamentally want. Although the need for an intimate bond is deeply embedded in all of us, we can be very content for significant periods of time with the company of close friends and a stimulating career.

However, being single still involves relating – whether to casual lovers or best friends. The 'single path' is explored in detail in Chapter 2, but strategies to improve relating in all kinds of ways are included throughout this book.

If the answer to 'Are you sure you want a relationship?' is an unqualified 'Yes!', you still need to take a moment to reflect on whether you feel ready to take on the responsibility for such a big leap in your life right now.

If you do feel ready, remember that just waiting around won't make anything happen; you will only make this leap by tackling things differently and by taking charge of your future. If you yearn for action, don't give any ground to inertia or procrastination. If you want things to stay the same, then well and good; if you don't, then look at how your initiatives today can be the catalyst for a new and more exciting life tomorrow.

A good starting point is to understand much more clearly what you want from a relationship. Try the following Mansearch Checklist:

Mansearch Checklist – Knowing what you want

How do you see your ideal relationship? If you could wave a magic wand, would it be:

Check

An intimate togetherness with marriage/cohabitation?	☐
A part-time but committed lover?	☐
Together but independent?	☐
Friend and lover?	☐
Together and sharing the joys of children?	☐
Other preferences:	☐

....

Today, unlike in times gone by, there are many models of happy relationships to consider. But remember, whatever transpires in real life will never be exactly what you anticipate; adjustments and compromises are nearly always necessary. Nevertheless, having a model of what you'd ideally like is important for keeping you motivated. Being aware of what is blocking the realization of this ideal will take away the power of that block and enable you to start being proactive.

Soundbyte

> Opinion polls reveal that on one thing, at least, males and females do agree – that the most important ingredient for potential partnership is: 'That we both make each other laugh'.

The Smart Biogs that follow will help you identify tendencies or situations of which you may be unaware but which could get in the way of your search for a good relationship. Can you recognize any of their experiences in your own life history? If so, do underline the relevant bits. These will help you with later

Workouts. The stories are mostly from women who joined Drawing Down the Moon, and LoveandFriends.com. Naturally, identities have been changed to protect their privacy.

SMART BIOG: **Sophie and the bio-clock**

Sophie was a humorous and articulate 36-year-old solicitor. University-educated and pretty, she had a demanding job in commercial litigation, a lively circle of friends and plenty of interests. She was not the sort of woman you'd expect to have trouble finding a lover, but she did. In an otherwise full life, she felt there was a void – and time was getting on.

Three or four years before this meeting, Sophie had felt it was time to start a family. However, George, her partner at that time, would only repeat that he wasn't ready, at least not yet, and he refused to talk about it further. For Sophie, the longing increased and the day before her 36th birthday she blew a fuse and walked out. They tried to patch things up, but Sophie felt she had to stand her ground and look after her own needs. She believed that if she was to have children it was now or never. And so with a heavy heart, she left George for good.

That was several months before she came to see me and, in the meantime, there hadn't been even the glimpse of an interesting, eligible man, let alone a broody one. 'Ten years ago, I had no problem,' she lamented. 'Men seemed to be everywhere. Where have they all gone? All my women friends are having the same experience.'

Keynotes for Sophie

Obviously one can't fight the bio-clock. Sophie needed to maximize her exposure to dating opportunities but, paradoxically, she also had to put the baby issue on the back burner. There is nothing so scary to men as broody-women-in-a-hurry. They often come across as desperate and merely looking for a stud.

What happened? After joining Drawing Down the Moon, Sophie began to have so much fun on her dates that she relaxed and almost forgot about beating her bio-clock. Once that pressure was off, to her surprise eligible men started popping up everywhere in her life. Why? Having such a plethora of dates made her feel great and consequently made her more attractive. She met Nigel, 'The One', not through my agency but on a public speaking course they both enrolled for.

SMART BIOG: **Claire: no time, never here – and there's the baby**

Claire was one of Sophie's friends. In fact, she had recommended Sophie to the agency. She, herself, had joined a month earlier. She was 33-years old and the business-development manager for an up-and-coming software company. A warm, slightly husky voice alerted me to the possibility that she might be a smoker – this could make her more difficult to match. Her relationship – with David, whom she had seen three or four times a week but had never lived with – had continued till her work took her to Japan for some months. Then, in spite of attempts to sustain it by phone, texting, fax and e-mail, it ground to a halt.

At the time of the break-up, she found she was pregnant but decided to carry on as a single parent. She gave birth to a baby boy whom she named Chris. Since then, she had been wondering why she no longer met men whom she considered relationship material. Her circle of friends seemed to have coalesced almost imperceptibly into couples with children. She told me that her work still often took her overseas and that her schedule was hectic. She was frequently up at 6 am to feed Chris before leaving him with the baby-minder or the au pair and going on to the office. After coming home from work, she again had Chris to consider, despite the domestic help – and David caring for him every other weekend.

It was no surprise to hear that somehow the baby and job always took precedence over her social life. She had been out with two or three men since Chris had been born but she wasn't in the mood to pursue anything.

I pointed out to Claire that making more space for her private life should now be on her critical list of things to do. To create this space, she had to learn to say 'No' to some of the demands her company made of her, without jeopardizing her position. This would be difficult, but the important things in life shouldn't always have to give way to matters that *others* regard as urgent. Could she negotiate with David to care for Chris one night a week, in addition to alternate weekends, so that she could go out? And, what about the smoking? Even smokers don't want to meet other smokers in the agency – they know they'll have no incentive to quit.

She took a half-full pack of cigarettes from her bag and threw them in my bin. 'That's it', she said, 'I've had my last fag'. True to her word she never had another.

But it wasn't until she had actually started dating with us and realized that there could be life apart from her work/baby tug-of-war that she felt courageous enough to tackle her boss about delegating some of her tasks and working partly from home. It was never going to be easy, but she made the time to date through us nearly every couple of weeks and indeed she eventually met her man – Adrian, a 32-year-old TV scriptwriter and aspiring novelist. She told me that she was only his second date, but he was her seventeenth. Worth waiting for? You bet!

SMART BIOG: Caroline and the workplace-romance myth

Caroline, 27, was a hard-working investigative journalist on a national newspaper. In fact, she had a suitor there – her editor, John. However, she knew she had to fend off his advances because if they were seen to be too friendly, people would say she had only got promotion because she was sleeping with him.

However, in a job like hers, surely she would be meeting lots of people outside the office when she was interviewing for articles, and there had to be some potential partners amongst them? 'No,' she told me. 'When I go out on a story, I have to appear to be really interested in the people I interview, which often flatters and fascinates them. But then I have to write an objective piece, which may put them off. Anyway, the next day I'm on to another job, so there's no possibility of anything developing. I'm fed up with work preventing me from meeting my future partner – I hope you can help.'

Wised-up women in Caroline's position know the dangers of workplace romance and have nothing to do with it. She needed to use her well-honed professional investigative skills to research all her alternative options, and there are many. Not only did Caroline join the Agency and also loveandFriends.com, and she also started going to wine-tastings (my suggestion) all of which provided lots of dating opportunities. At the time of writing she is seeing a lot of Greg, an English professor we matched her up with.

L♡vebyte

❝ The hardest task of a girl's life is to prove to a man that his intentions are serious. ❞

Helen Roland, *Reflections of a Bachelor Girl*

SMART BIOG: **Alison and the single-sex job syndrome**

Alison, aged 27, was an existing agency member who'd come in for a review session. Hers was a different problem. She was a primary-school teacher, and so most of her colleagues were women – as were a lot of her friends. When she did socialize, it was mostly with other education and public-sector workers in a similar position. Teachers often have very little opportunity to meet people from other professional backgrounds – I know, having worked in education myself.

Alison was happy to report that, through a variety of introductions, we had solved her isolation problem. Now, however, she needed to overcome her tendency to rush into new relationships. She was looking for someone who would share her passion for animals and environmental issues. Recently she had been dating Stephen who worked in publishing and was a supporter of Greenpeace. She'd come in to discuss whether she should go 'on hold' because of him. (Going 'on hold' means we don't give any further introductions for the time being.) Alison felt there was some real chemistry between them and she wanted to see how the friendship would progress. But how, she wanted to know, could she ensure that she didn't sabotage the relationship, as she had done on previous occasions, by being too hasty and seeming too needy? Was it too soon to go on hold – and, if she did, should she tell him?

To be aware of the relationship-blockers is to win 99% of the battle. Alison now knew she had to stop and take a deep breath before she made any significant moves in her budding relationship or it might fizzle out as had happened before. She needed to tune in to whether Stephen himself was ready to take matters further and not make a big issue of going on hold because of him.

Alison said it really helped to know that there would always be plenty more men for her to meet through the agency if the future didn't work out with Stephen. So it was much easier for her to take it easy and not rush things. If it worked – wonderful. If it didn't at least she'd made a special friend and she could ring in and ask us for another introduction. Alison also took my advice and registered for a salsa class to spread her net even wider – just in case and to take the pressure off.

L♡vebyte

❝ Commitment is what every woman wants; men can't even spell it. ❞
Laura Zigman

SMART BIOG: **Susan – scarily successful**

Susan, aged 31, had come in to find out about joining the agency. She was clearly a successful high-achiever and I felt she might be a bit of a challenge.

The very perfectionist strategies that pave the way to the top for such women may often undermine their search for a mate. 'I have my own house and car,' she told me. 'I'm in charge of a sales force of 150. I've got where I am through knowing what I want. But now I realize that there's a part of my life that doesn't match up to the rest. I never seem to meet men who come up to my standard. I've been out on lots of first and second dates and have found I can't take them any further. I find it impossible to meet a man my equal – someone I can respect, let alone love.'

Her friends were always telling her that she was hypercritical and should realize that no one is perfect. I pointed out, as I always do to potential members, that the person she was likely to end up with would probably defy most of her preconceptions. She needed to make allowances for this or she would rule out all possibilities before a relationship got off the ground.

Susan conceded that if she had been less judgmental, perhaps a good relationship could have developed with one of the men she had previously met, but she didn't realize it at the time. This admission exposed a chink in her armour. At least that she was now aware of the problem. The main challenges for Susan were to work hard to become much more flexible and to relax and take more emotional risks. She had to be prepared to explore any relationship that had something positive about it. Going on just three or four dates with a man to find out more about him isn't tantamount to commitment. She just needed to be clear that it didn't signify more than it was.

Susan seemed to think that finding a man was a bit like interviewing a new salesperson: she judged them on the strength of one or two 'interviews' and they either passed or failed – and most of them failed. But life isn't like that when it comes to relationships. Recognizing the right person also depends on oneself and one's own readiness. Relationships are built over time and not just found – Susan still had to learn this and she said she'd try.

So it was with a degree of apprehension that I signed her up for Drawing Down the Moon. Would she break lots of hearts I wondered? Well, she did, but they mended. After about 10 months Susan told me that Doug – one of her earliest dates, who had become 'just a good friend' over the months that she knew him – had suddenly become rather attractive to her. Some months later a card arrived from Thailand: 'Just thought you ought to know that we got married! Thanks a million – Love Doug and Susan'.

S⊚undbyte

When you next find yourself saying: 'I always know within the first 30 seconds whether I am going to fancy him or not', bear in mind that 62% of the men and 73% of the women questioned on the subject said they now found their current partner more attractive than when they first met.

SMART BIOG: Alex – off-puttingly affluent

Alex's life seemed an enviable one. At 44, and the owner of her own recruitment company, she had a high income and a great social life. She was feminine, stylish and bubbly. Her easy manner and sense of humour made it difficult to understand how anyone could find her intimidating. 'I always have to play down my financial success,' she explained. 'A lot of men find it off-putting. Choosing holidays and restaurants with a man who earns less than I do is embarrassing. I need to meet someone who shares my lifestyle and income level and is at least my equal in energy and intellect.'

Because she wanted her future partner to be an exceptionally high-flyer, this narrowed Alex's field considerably. She had found her problem compounded by the fact that men who were attractive, rich and successful had a charismatic allure for certain younger women – those whom the more cynical might call 'trophy women'. It is one of life's unquestionable facts that men can be shorter, balder and older but all this fades dramatically next to the appeal of power and success. Alex was having to 'compete' with a large age-span of women for a small group of men. Her task needed to be tackled on many fronts simultaneously to ensure success.

The outcome for Alex? Because she was in an age group that suffers from a shortage of men and she was very, very selective, we suggested we should harness the volume element of internet dating to the selectiveness of a personal introduction agency and register her for our bespoke **Personal Matchmaker membership**. Alex had no time to pursue the more labour intensive route of internet dating and anyway she felt more secure with her dates being pre-selected. Together we would cherry pick a shortlist of attractive men from the thousands on the internet dating site I co-owned, LoveandFriends.com and we would invite them in to Drawing Down the Moon to be personally interviewed and identity checked. The ones we thought suitable we would introduce to Alex. At the time of writing Alex is meeting the first men we've selected for her. Her response? 'It's staggering – I never thought so many interesting, high-calibre men existed. Chemistry? – ask me in six months'.

Loosen up

Do these cases press any buttons for you? Have you underlined any similarities with your own situation? My colleagues and I hear stories in this vein every day, many times over. It never ceases to be a surprise, even to me, that these superbly attractive women find it so difficult to meet someone for a relationship. As I've said, it is sometimes difficult to separate the social factors that have brought about their predicaments from the emotions that their problem generates. For these women, relationships have become a tough hurdle in a challenging obstacle race created by too rapid a change in society. They need to adapt quickly if they are not to be left behind.

This is where a flexible and novel approach reaps dividends. Be brave. If past strategies haven't worked, learn from the failures and try new ones. Experiment and have fun!

L♡vebyte

** Courtship: a man pursuing a woman until she catches him. **
Anon

Practise till you purr-rr-rr

It has always struck me that most books about finding a partner are too theoretical. They don't focus enough on the value of practice and more practice. There isn't enough guidance on concrete steps that can be taken to maximize opportunities. What use are greater insights into developing a relationship if you don't have anybody around to have a decent relationship with? What use is a new recipe if you lack the raw ingredients – in the shape of at least a couple of tasty men? The more dates you have, the less emotionally needy and more relaxed you will become – and the more attractive you will be to others. It's that Domino Dating effect again – knock one hurdle down and all the rest go with it. So, with all the expertise you deploy for other areas of your life, start creating a variety of new dating opportunities – Smart Dating will show you how.

Mansearch Workouts

Let's get started on the Mansearch Workouts. Try and do this first one thoughtfully. Think of why you want to go into a relationship. And do you really want one? Be honest. Give yourself plenty of time.

Mansearch Workout – Getting under way

My reasons for wanting to be in a relationship (list in order of priority):

1) ....

2) ....

3) ....

4) ....

5) ....

And as many more reasons as you can think of:

....

....

Any surprises? Are these the reasons you went into your last relationship? Are they powerful enough to make you want to change anything in your present single state?

Let's disentangle the elements of your particular situation. Why aren't you dating if you really want a relationship? Put social factors on one side for a minute and ask yourself if there is anything you feel that is holding you back from your search for a partner? Coming to recognize any sabotaging strategies that you are using is the first step to ensuring you have more control over your destiny. The Mansearch Workouts will help you to do this systematically by encouraging you to have a dialogue with yourself about various problem areas. Greater awareness of issues and problems is an essential precondition for action.

In the next Mansearch Checklist, compile for yourself a list of the reasons why you are not meeting, or perhaps even seeking out, potentially eligible single men at the moment. This will be another useful record you can use to help you see how your feelings, thought processes, and experiences are changing as you read through *Smart Dating*.

Mansearch Checklist – My top 10 ways of never getting started on finding a partner

Are you:

Check

Blocking opportunities for meeting interesting men because you are nervous of being rejected or hurt? ☐

Apprehensive about offending a man by not 'falling in love' with him? ☐

Finding that work has taken over too much recently and is squeezing out the energy and the opportunities needed? ☐

Never able to fancy men who fancy you? ☐

Frightened of losing control? ☐

Waiting for your children to grow older before you let a new man into your life? ☐

Telling yourself it is because you haven't 'met the right one' yet? ☐

Thinking that there are simply no decent, single men available? ☐

Finding it hard to 'lower your high standards' enough to give any man a chance? ☐

Other reasons for not getting started: ☐

....

Workout – identifying your relationship blockers

Any of us can have something that holds us back from taking action, and to minimize its power over us we need to confront it. What, in your present situation, is blocking change – the change from being in a single state to a relationship one? Tackle the next Workout in a light-hearted manner and see if anything useful emerges for you to incorporate into your Finding-a-Partner Plan.

Apart from gaining much insight from the entries themselves – the reasons you put down for not being in a relationship at the moment – with this next Workout you will be gaining extra knowledge by further analysing your answers quickly and effectively.

Circumstantial blockers

Put a tick in the **Circumstantial** checkbox if you consider the particular reason for not being in a relationship is situational and not to do with you personally – for example, if you believe that the reason is the shortage of available men in your age group.

Psychological blockers

Tick the **Psychological** checkbox if you think the reason is to do with your personality and your degree of readiness for a relationship – for example, do you always choose unavailable men? Some reasons, such as 'I'm always away on business', may be both circumstantial and psychological. For instance, you may have chosen a particular situation, such as a career involving lots of travel (which makes partnerships difficult), as a passive resistance against settling into a relationship.

Other **Psychological** checkbox ticks might be for matters such as 'I keep making bad decisions about relationships – they're usually too short-sighted' or 'My ideas about relationships aren't keeping up with these fast-moving times'. Or maybe you're only choosing men because they are sexually attractive with no regard to their suitability as a long-term partner.

Physical Blockers

Does the **Physical** checkbox need ticking for you – is the way you look sabotaging your best chances? Do you need a presentation makeover because you have let yourself go physically? Would a good diet, a regular gym routine and a shopping spree give you extra confidence and oomph?

Habit Blockers

You should tick the **Habits** checkbox if, for instance, you drink too much on dates or if you are a smoker (a big date deterrent, by the way).

Change blockers

Tick the **Change** checkbox if the reason is something you'd like to change. For example, you may need to work on yourself because you believe, 'I frighten men off'. Or perhaps it is a question of meeting only the wrong sort of men? The two problems may be distinct in concept but overlap a lot in practice. Are you the sort of person who never gets past the first or second date? Is this because you are rejecting the men at this point, or are they rejecting you – or perhaps both? In reality you are more likely to emerge with a cluster of related causes than one clear reason that can be tackled on its own.

Mansearch Workout – Reasons why you don't currently meet available, single men

Nothing's happening right now because (write your reasons below):

	Circumstantial?	Psychological?	Physical?	Habits?	Change?
1)	☐	☐	☐	☐	☐
2)	☐	☐	☐	☐	☐
3)	☐	☐	☐	☐	☐
4)	☐	☐	☐	☐	☐
5)	☐	☐	☐	☐	☐

And as many more reasons as you can think of:

....

First relationship blockers to go are ...

Now take your list from the Workout and, for the next Workout, *include only those reasons for not being in a relationship that you have the power to change or to which you could adapt!* Put all the things you cannot change onto the back-burner, neither to be ignored but not to focus on nor feel bitter about. As you read through the book, see if your approach to this exercise changes. Make notes in your **Action and Success Diary** (see page 21) of what you think as you go. These will form the basis of your own Relationship Action Plan.

Mansearch Workout – Relationship blockers

The relationship blockers which I have the power to change or to which I could adapt are:

1) ....

2) ....

3) ....

4) ....

5) ....

And as many more reasons as you can think of:

....

....

L♡vebyte

❝ If you don't get everything you want, think of the things you don't get that you don't want. ❞
Oscar Wilde

Workout and Action-Plan Strategies

Starting as you mean to go on

The point of writing such definitive lists so early on is to have them at hand when you are working through the other chapters. As you read on, I'd like you to review and amend them repeatedly, incorporating new ideas as you feel your way. You may find some powerful feelings emerging in relation to particular aspects of the Workouts; these may be familiar to you, or they may be surprising and painful. Just be prepared to take them all on board.

Feeling your way

Strong feelings, properly acknowledged and worked through, can be great motivation for change.

Positive feedback

Some women find it helpful to talk things through with friends as they work through this sort of programme. However, a word of warning! Moan-and-misery sessions have their place and can be cathartic, and from time to time they can help to clear the system. But my experience is that overindulgence in this area is best avoided because it can be counterproductive.

We need to associate with positive and upbeat people when planning a change in our lives. Negative people will say there is no point looking for a relationship because, for example, 'Men simply don't come up to women's standards' or 'Men just aren't prepared to commit themselves' – and so on. So, seek out the optimists and give the pessimists a wide berth!

Your Action and Success Diary

Write down your thoughts, feelings and achievements in a special Action and Success Diary every night. This will help you to have productive internal conversations with yourself and to prepare your Relationship Action Plan to decide what you are going to do the next day. This Action Plan is going to be the step-by-step, stage-by-stage blueprint and record for your Dating Programme and your Partner Hunt. This way you can keep closely focused on the goal of building a relationship with someone special.

Get yourself a Dating Buddy

To help focus your energy and intent, ask a supportive and optimistic friend or relative to be your **Dating Buddy**. Show them your Workouts and tell them your plans for action. Fill them in on the goals and strategies involved by giving them this book to read. If they are in the same situation as you are, you could support each other.

Enter into a firm agreement to phone your Dating Buddy every week at an appointed time for a half-hour chat to update them on your progress. At the end of each phone session, you must make a commitment to undertake **three**

positive moves towards your goals during the next few days – moves which you will report back on the following week – and enter these on your Relationship Action Plan (*see below*). 'In-between' phone calls are great if that is not imposing on your Dating Buddy too much.

Ask your Dating Buddy to be constructive and supportive at all times. Also, ask them to try always to hold off negative criticism until it can be put in a positive context. It's a big responsibility for someone to help you in this way, so do make sure they know that you appreciate what they are doing for you. They will help you pick yourself up when you are down and point out how to avoid past pitfalls. With their support you should travel further and faster.

If you prefer not to enlist a Dating Buddy, or there's no one available to ask, focus your motivation by spending more time on your Action and Success Diary.

And now, on to your Keynotes & Diary Prompts, your first Relationship Action Plan and then – your well-earned TREATS.

Keynotes & Diary Prompts

1 If you are a busy professional, recognize that you may also have to work hard to find and build a relationship.
2 Identify any psychological tendencies you have which could sabotage finding a relationship.
3 List any circumstantial reasons that may be blocking your chances of making a relationship.
4 Plan lifestyle changes to create more time for meeting potential partners.
5 Avoid being around negative people who disparage the idea of looking for a relationship.
6 Seek out positive, happy companions who'll act as inspiring role models and encourage you with your Relationship Action Plan.
7 Set up your Action and Success Dating Diary on your organizer.
8 Recruit your Dating Buddy.
9 Take some immediate steps to get your Relationship Action Plan moving.

RELATIONSHIP ACTION PLAN 1

Note down your Smart Action points for the next week.

Positive Action 1:

....

....

Positive Action 2:

....

....

Positive Action 3:

....

....

Treats

While we're on the subject of being positive, to boost your motivation and self esteem give yourself a TREAT, right now, before you read Chapter 2. This can simply be:

♡ a cup of real coffee, or

♡ a glass of good wine, or you could

♡ ring a cheerful friend for a gossip. After all – you deserve it!

♡ find a lovely notebook/diary for your Action and Success Diary in which you can record your Positive Dating Actions and Results – and the dates for your next Mansearch Steps. However, use any notebook or piece of paper to be going on with or, of course, your personal organizer or computer.

He doesn't have to be as classically handsome as George Clooney – someone like Brad Pitt would do.

chapter 2

Super-Single or Super-Mate?

Getting a buzz from independence

Forget about your quest for a significant other for a moment. Let's look at the *joys* and *advantages* of being unattached and then imagine how great it would be if you could also enjoy most of these in a relationship! What's the secret?

I believe that being properly single at some stage is a 'must' if you want to discover yourself and be a positive, independent-minded human being. As long as you have a good social life, being on your own can be an enriching experience that enables you to set priorities. You'll have more to offer if you do go into a relationship and you'll know what you want out of it. When you finally embark on your adventure in togetherness, you'll bring strength to the new relationship and the individuality of each of you will be all the more enhanced. After the break-up of any kind of partnership, it is especially good to have a spell by yourself. It can be tough, but it's certainly better than rushing, with all your emotional neediness, straight into a new relationship. Look around you: happy singles make happy couples!

L♡vebyte

" The day he moved out was terrible –
That evening she went through hell.
His absence wasn't the problem
But the corkscrew had gone as well. **"**
Wendy Cope, 'Loss'

Let's look at some ways in which singledom, partnership, individuality and dependence mesh together and influence the way relationships turn out. When reading the **Smart Biogs** throughout this book, have a think about these four elemental 'life modes'. Try and imagine how the advantages of each of them could work for you without the disadvantages. Crack this and you'll find your next relationship a lot more rewarding.

SMART BIOG: **Clinging Marion finds her own feet**

Marion, a 31-year-old dentist, had split up from Roger nine months before she came to see us about joining the agency. They'd been living together for three years in his house. It had been a really passionate relationship and they did everything together. She missed him dreadfully when they were apart and even phoned him every day at work just to say 'I love you' and ask 'Do you miss me?' Roger's colleagues were bemused by his metamorphosis from dynamic banker into gooey lovebird when he was talking to her. The couple behaved almost as if they had to prove to the world that they were made for each other.

All their friends anticipated they'd marry and they both felt they were travelling in that direction. Then one of Roger's old flames reappeared on the scene. He found that he was drawn back towards her and, rather abruptly, he asked Marion to leave. She was devastated, and her first angry feelings of betrayal were not just about Roger but about men in general: they were obviously a species not to be trusted.

In spite of herself, or perhaps to spite the opposite sex, she had a couple of one-night stands after parties where well-meaning friends had introduced her to men they knew. The split had happened so quickly that she didn't know what she wanted to do. She rented a flat from a friend who was working abroad and moved in – alone for the first time in her life. At first she just cried herself sick; after that she began spending as much time as possible with friends or talking on the phone to anyone who'd lend an ear.

Then, one Saturday, after a week of working late with her accounts and paperwork, it dawned on her that she'd got nothing fixed up for that night. To her amazement, she felt quite exhilarated at the prospect of an evening all to herself. How should she spend it? For the first time since she moved in, she springcleaned the flat – and this gave her great satisfaction. She went out and did an arduous session at the gym and, on her way home, visited the local Italian deli and bought all her favourite foods. After getting back, she ran a bath, soaked for ages and had an evening of personal indulgence and relaxation. There were no tears, no telephone calls and no trusty friends to distract her: just herself alone, in her space, in her time. She realized she was on the road to recovery.

During the next few months, Marion continued to enjoy socializing but began to do more things on her own. She explained to me that she now knew that she had become so dependent on Roger that her identity had been swallowed up by his. Consequently, she had been unable to appreciate herself fully. She also became aware that Roger had felt somewhat smothered by their relationship but didn't know how to express this. The nine months on her own had been empowering. In fact, she was almost happy with the idea of remaining single for some time; she no longer felt the need to confirm her worth by living in a partnership. Yet, like most people, she preferred being in – and staying with – a relationship.

I suggested to Marion that she continue to pay attention to developing her own strengths and special qualities whilst exploring her quest for a relationship. Her tendency to be dependent needed to be counterbalanced by encouraging more independent characteristics. She needed no prompting. Over the succeeding months you could say she blossomed and perhaps because of this she became attractive to a different type of man. She discovered a more independent, but intimate, love affair with Leon. And I haven't heard from them since. No news is good news.

Your special-qualities Workout

This is the point where it would be useful for you to focus on your own qualities as a single, complete-in-your-own-right person and a 'woman of character' – not just as someone who is single, unattached and waiting to go into a relationship. Do this for the next **Workout**. Don't underrate yourself, you are special – everything about you is unique! Below are a few suggestions – many of which DO apply to you. Make sure your list is *much* longer than this one.

What are your gifts and talents? Are you, for instance:

♡   a talented professional;

♡   a wonderful friend;

♡   an encouraging optimist;

♡   a passionate lover;

♡   a fine cook;

♡   a sympathetic listener;

♡   an empowering employer;

♡   a supportive employee;

♡   an excellent hostess;

♡   a relaxing companion;

♡   a keen walker;

♡   an enthusiastic concert-goer;

♡   a great joke-teller.

This is an important exercise. Take the time to appreciate yourself fully and honourably.

Mansearch Workout – Your gifts and talents

My drop-dead-fantastic-qualities CV includes:

1) ....

2) ....

3) ....

4) ....

5) ....

And as many more gifts and talents as you can think of:
....
....

A couple – two halves or two wholes?

Throughout history, simply in order to survive, people have nearly always had to live in some sort of group. In most societies it has been difficult for women to own property and live independently. As late as the 1960s, a woman couldn't usually take out a mortgage or even hire a television in Britain without a man acting as guarantor. Professional women in the West now take it for granted that they will be responsible for themselves and buy or rent their own homes, cars, pensions and holidays. Indeed, I still remember the exhilaration of walking through my own front door for the first time.

It is, at last, economically viable for women to live alone from choice, and many women feel good about being single for a substantial chunk of their lives. They know this doesn't mean they are psychologically stunted or unable to make relationships. Not so long ago, most women would have felt that they were incomplete without their 'other half'. The word 'spinster' has always had negative connotations of on-the-shelf failure, whereas 'bachelor' has virile associations and is seen in a much more positive light.

In spite of media messages urging coupledom, many women have blossomed into emotional and economic self-sufficiency without a partner. This means that when two people do decide to come together, it's a fusion of two wholes rather than two halves. This seems to be one of the keys to a happy and more fulfilled relationship.

Stuck in a single rut?

What, however, might be the 'downsides' of being one of the 'proud to be single' lobby? One is that you might become somewhat selfish in your mission to be uncompromisingly independent. Also, you might begin to think that it's only through sacrificing your freedom that you can have an intimate relationship.

With the extraordinary rise of single households in recent years, people are tending to spend more time on their own than before. Could you, as a result, get too set in your ways? Might you become too fussy or even downright unrealistic about selecting a partner? Are you less able to adjust to the lifestyle changes necessitated by marriage or co-habitation – no matter how much you yearn for emotional fulfilment? How successful you are in dealing with this adjustment will depend on your strengths as an individual as well as your approach to communication. The really strong, sensitive and fulfilled woman who is also a good communicator can be a happy single or a happy partner. It's your choice: develop your strengths or indulge your weaknesses.

L♡vebyte

" A woman without a man is like a fish without a bicycle. **"**
   Gloria Steinem

Although being single is no longer automatically viewed as a state of incompleteness, most singles do eventually want to be in a relationship. However, this wish may come with conditions that can, if you don't watch yourself, escalate in proportion to the length of time you've been on your own. 'I'm certainly not desperate for commitment. I'm happy just being me – I have a wonderful life!' declare most new women applicants to **Drawing Down the Moon** – as soon as they sit down in our offices. 'A committed relationship with a man would just be the icing on the cake – but he's got to be **absolutely** right. No compromises for me.' But is it ever as straightforward as this? Isn't this rather limiting?

S☮undbyte

A Mintel survey of 2,000 couples and 1,175 singles concluded that one in three singles was less happy than they used to be. The figure for couples was only 18%. More than half the over-35 singles were sadder than 5 years ago compared with only 39% of couples.

Live-out love: from his-and-her towels to his-and-her homes

Even if you are in a relationship, you might choose to live alone. An increasing number of couples practice 'live-out togetherness', maybe seeing each other for two or three days a week and going back to their own homes for the rest of the time. This may just continue until they get to know each other better, or, in some cases, it may be a permanent arrangement. This is in stark contrast to the 1970s and 1980s when everyone was rushing into co-habitation and perhaps marriage. So, living alone need not necessarily mean 'no partner'.

Live-out relationships are fine when a couple first get to know each another or when they aren't ready for co-habitation or marriage; but perhaps they are more questionable when a couple are living apart on a long-term basis *only because* they are unable to manage intimacy and closeness. However, to know that you are capable of intimacy but have a live-out relationship simply from choice – and when children aren't on the agenda – is, of course, fine. In fact, many older people whose offspring have flown the nest may choose this option – albeit, on a permanent, committed basis.

SMART BIOG: Roberta – living apart and drifting apart

Let's look at 35-year-old Roberta. Initially, she had phoned me from New York where she had been living for four years while working for an international entertainment organization. She told me about her last important relationship. She had chosen not to move in with Ian, who lived two streets away in New York, even after their affair started to get serious. In fact, she found it much more fun having him round for the weekend, or rushing over to his place for the night. The apartment she was renting was stunning and she had a terrific social life. After three years, they started to drift apart. She realized it was all finally over when she was offered a senior post at her company's London office and she grabbed it with both hands.

Nevertheless, the pair stayed firm friends and in fact it was Ian who suggested that it might be an idea for Roberta to line up an introduction agency in London before she came back to England. Many of his friends in New York had used agencies and lonely-hearts advertisements with great success. These are much more a part of people's lives in the USA than in Britain, although the Brits are beginning to catch on.

Roberta was in no rush to find Mr Perfect. She just wanted to ensure that she had a great social life and plenty of men to meet when she came over. However, she hoped that at some point she'd meet someone very special and settle down. 'And live together?' I asked. 'Well, maybe eventually, and certainly if we decided to have children, but it would have to be a pretty large home! I really enjoy my own space and don't like to share it much', she explained.

Demanding and selfish or open and receptive? It will depend on how she handles it. Roberta should watch that she doesn't become too inflexible – a perennial danger for successful singles who can so easily write off all potential partners as 'not for me'. I suggested that she attempt to cultivate more relationships that challenge her insularity and stretch her horizons. This is something that's easier to do in an introduction agency where one can explore exciting new connections with people one would never meet in everyday life.

L♡vebyte

" Absence sharpens love, presence strengthens it. **"**
Thomas Fuller (II), '*Gnomologia*' (1732)

Single and loving it!

Prepare for another Workout. Make a list of all the positive aspects for *you* of being on your own. This is a special list to be dated and kept safely, especially *after* you go into a relationship. Prune it occasionally (and only after much reflection) to encourage healthy growth through prioritizing. Refer to it to see how you can retain some of these positives if you go into a relationship.

I don't subscribe to the school of thought that believes self-sacrifice is necessary to build a relationship. Sensitivity, accommodation, negotiation and humour, yes – but self-sacrifice, no! I have observed that people in really happy relationships are those who value themselves and their own lives as much as those of their partner. The point of this Workout is to identify the things that you value about life as an *individual*, and not as *half of a couple*. You might want to include all or some of the following:

♡ more freedom;

♡ time to see your friends;

♡ control over all kinds of decision making, especially those concerned with money;

♡ privacy;

♡ feeling you can be more spontaneous.

Mansearch Workout – Reasons for being single

My 'single-and-loving-it!' essentials list is:

1) ....

2) ....

3) ....

4) ....

5) ....

And as many more reasons as you can think of:

....

....

Living-alone negatives

Now, move on to the next Workout, which is, as you may guess, looking at the downside of living alone. Which are the aspects you dread most and would willingly leave behind?

- ♡ no one to recount your day to;
- ♡ solo holidays;
- ♡ no one to share a laugh with;
- ♡ no sex on tap;
- ♡ being self-centred;
- ♡ no one to share responsibilities with.

Mansearch Workout – Reasons not to be single

The downsides for me of being single:

1) ....

2) ....

3) ....

4) ....

5) ....

And any others you can think of:

....

....

Are there any surprises here? How many of these are mundane and unimportant? Which ones are hell? Which are avoidable? Whereabouts, if at all, have you mentioned missing out on good sex? If you haven't, is it because you don't miss it, or is it that casual or solo sex can be as good for you? Have you included not having children, or do you feel that this is something that needn't always coincide with a relationship? Maybe you have children already and wish you had someone with whom you could share their good and bad times.

Independent – or just selfish?

Enjoying your independence is one thing, but becoming selfish is another. I think we are all aware of how quickly we lose any tolerance of other people's shortcomings when we are not in a relationship; how we begin to want arrangements to be made on our own terms. This can make us very reluctant to move in with someone else, especially if we have been in a bad relationship before, if we have lived alone for a long time, or simply if we are getting older and know well what we like best.

As in all situations, it's best to be aware of potential problems – then they can get less of a grip on us. When I was learning Transcendental Meditation, I came across a useful metaphor for being aware of, but not bugged by, difficulties. It was: 'Tiptoe around the sleeping elephants'. This is how you can deal with the downsides of being single. Take notice, but negotiate around them. If you know that you are single from choice, not necessity, then it will be a pleasure so to be.

L♡vebyte

" To love oneself is the beginning of a lifelong romance. **"**
Oscar Wilde

Advantages of being in a relationship

Before focusing on how to avoid the disadvantages of being in a relationship, why not use this next **Workout** to remind yourself of the advantages.

Mansearch Workout – Relationship advantages

The pluses of partnership are:

1) ....

2) ....

3) ....

4) ....

5) ....

And any others you can think of:

....

....

You may have mentioned:

♡ companionship;

♡ someone to cheer you up when you're down;

♡ good sex;

♡ someone to share joys and sorrows with;

♡ someone to talk to about your day;

♡ sharing expenses.

Keep reminding yourself that the point of thinking about and compiling these lists is to see how the advantages of being in a relationship and the advantages of being single can be persuaded to cohabit happily.

Joys you missed in your last relationship

What did you *really* miss from your single life when you were in your last relationship? Where were you short-changed? Be scrupulously honest. Now, think, what could you do to avoid this happening next time round. See what this next Workout reveals.

Mansearch Workout – Shortcomings of your last relationship

My last relationship lacked:

1) ....

2) ....

3) ....

4) ....

5) ....

And any other shortcomings that you can think of:

....

....

Perhaps you:

♡ felt trapped;

♡ found you weren't motivated to see your friends;

♡ became involved in conflicts over decision making;

♡ yearned for more privacy;

♡ found you were less spontaneous.

Blending the best of singledom and togetherness

So that you can focus on being both a happy single and a happy partner, the next task is to compare the two lists of joys – single and partnership – to see where there are clashes. For example, you might find that autonomy in money matters is important to you and yet the appeal of shared, and thus reduced, expenses involves some sharing of responsibility too. Now think how you can resolve this if the situation arises – maybe a joint bank account just for household expenses *and* two personal ones.

Spending time on your own may be vitally important for you. It would need to be discussed and balanced against other needs in a relationship so that your partner doesn't feel rejected. Are you good at sorting out these kinds of issues both in relaxed and stressful situations? In what areas do you need more practice?

Taking care of my needs, your needs – and our needs

Relationships and marriage are more difficult to enter into than ever before. Today, we are so used to having our needs met instantly – whether by ordering take-away meals or clicking the remote control – that, if the same thing fails to happen in a relationship, we kick up a fuss. Nowadays, in complex Western societies, relationships depend much more on emotional need-fulfilment than they used to, and these needs are harder to meet than ever. Quality time together is at a premium, with careers, gym, travel, moving house and other time-hungry tasks taking over. Unless good communication about emotional needs is established early on in the relationship, established patterns can be difficult to adjust when real trouble looms.

L♡vebyte

❝ My mother said it was simple to keep a man - you must be a maid in the
living-room, a cook in the kitchen and a whore in the bedroom. I said
I'd hire the other two and take care of the bedroom bit. **❞**
Jerry Hall

The satisfaction surfers

The people whom I term 'satisfaction surfers' are those who chase an instant-
gratification type of lifestyle with such enthusiasm that they get scared when
an emerging relationship signals that some of it might have to go. As a result,
many develop a deep passive resistance to the concept of coupledom, and
unconsciously evade making a commitment even when part of them yearns for
closeness and intimacy. In spite of the evidence that shows that couples are, in
general, happier than singles, we find that people are putting off commitment
till later and later in life. Does this sound like you?

Creative couplings – that special chemistry

Although two people are more likely to communicate well if they have lots in
common, many lively relationships thrive on richness, diversity and a high level
of individuality. This sort of coupling is likely to be much more interesting and
creative, but these very virtues can also fuel deep disagreements and problems
if not well-handled.

In the old days, relationships were based more on an economic or dynastic
nexus. Today, it is the quality of the emotional interaction that is critical to
their survival. I think we seek more 'spark' in a potential partner than ever
before. So much more is expected, even demanded, in a 21st-century relationship that there is a stronger need for good negotiating skills right from the
start. These are an essential ingredient if that special chemistry between two
people is not to vanish when conflicts arise over having children, moving
homes, managing careers and taking on mortgages.

We can all improve the way we negotiate if we are prepared to learn and practise. The secret of success is to rehearse handling disagreements about the
colour of the bathroom before you start on the serious issues, such as whether
you're ready to have children.

I have noticed that those who most fear losing the advantages of being single are those who are the least assertive. By 'assertive' I mean expressing your opinions and needs clearly while respecting those of the other person. For instance, lots of people are very assertive at work and in certain social contexts, but when it comes to an intimate relationship, they find this difficult. They may, instead, have a tendency to become aggressive, passive or manipulative, or (most likely) to swing between these modes. Certain sorts of situations may trigger some inappropriate response learned in early life. If one of these situations arises with someone you love, then it can have unfortunate consequences.

SMART BIOG: **First-aid for oversensitive Veronica**

Veronica – 37, an interior designer – told me that she used to find that criticism of any of her actions felt like criticism of her as a person. Instead of being able to handle a negative comment about something fairly straightforward, such as her suggestion for a holiday, she would lash out with angry and violent retorts. Her husband, Robin, whom she loved dearly, became increasingly nervous of her outbursts, especially after the occasion when she got so angry she threw a hot iron at him. A friend pointed out to her that her overreactions could perhaps benefit from some professional help. Veronica knew she had to do something or her marriage would be on the rocks, so she enrolled on a 12-week Assertiveness Training course that the friend had just completed and recommended strongly.

Veronica found that Assertiveness Training is perhaps misleadingly named: 'training' sounded like something you do to dogs or roses, and 'assertiveness' hinted at aggression. With surprise and relief she discovered that, to the contrary, it is about being more in touch with feelings, values and opinions – your own and other peoples' – and about communicating these effectively and sensitively. It is about respecting your own and others' rights, expressing and receiving anger and criticism constructively. Above all, it is empowering and enables you to make choices.

The Assertiveness course helped Veronica realize that there were alternative responses she could use when criticized. She learned through role play how to express negative feelings sensitively in simple conflict situations so that they didn't get bottled up and explode later on as total character demolition. Role play? It sounds scary, but, working with a small group of people, she learned first to 'disclose' feelings and thus 'set the scene'. The first feeling to emerge from each person in the group was that they were terrified of role play! This disclosure immediately united them in solidarity and defused the tension. They had a good laugh and plunged into the simple structured exercises without further ado.

With practice and kindly but helpful feedback from each other, they learned and relearned new strategies for communicating in tricky situations. The idea is only to role play the less threatening issues at the beginning: the 'ones', 'twos' and 'threes', as they were called, and reserve the 'eights', 'nines' and 'tens' till they felt really confident. Soon, Veronica's initial apprehension dissolved and she found communication 'mountains' became mere 'molehills'. Not only could she take her clients' criticisms less defensively, but those of Robin, too.

The course leader also put Veronica in touch with a psychotherapist who she then visited for some time to talk through her situation. Just the fact that she'd made an effort to confront her problems led to a much calmer atmosphere at home. She found she could handle her negative feelings in a more positive and less destructive way, and the regular outbursts became something of the past. Veronica and Robin soon found that their relationship was back on track and even decided to treat their next holiday as a second honeymoon. Indeed, Robin was so impressed by Veronica's new-found confidence that he enrolled on an Assertiveness-Training course himself; he felt it might help him deal with his overbearing boss – and it did! He even agreed to see a couples' counsellor with Veronica – this had been suggested by her therapist as the next step.

That scary magic called closeness

Of course, cases are rarely as extreme as that of Veronica and Robin. I've reduced theirs to its essentials and shared it with you because it illustrates that particular problem so well. However, when people have difficulties resolving differences in a relationship and cannot express themselves clearly and considerately, then they may feel that the problem lies in the other person and not themselves. They will increasingly come to fear closeness and feel that the only way their needs will be met is to stay single. So strong is this fear that some people almost turn their independence into a philosophy of life. As a result, they tend to emit strong 'keep clear' messages to any potential partners they may meet.

Doormat or dominatrix?

Most of us do express ourselves effectively much of the time, but we all have some emotional no-go areas that could benefit from a more assertive approach. It is usually these that fuel the trouble in a relationship. There is probably an assertiveness course available near you. Why not check it out? It may be the best all-round investment you can make in your own future.

In the Mansearch Checklist below are some examples of situations where choosing an assertive approach (as opposed to 'doormat demeanour' or 'indirect manipulation') will make all the difference. Tick any of the ones that you tend to have difficulties with – whether in everyday life or in a close relationship.

Mansearch Checklist – Difficulties in asserting yourself

I have difficulties asserting myself (appropriately) when:

Check

♡ **Expressing feelings** ☐
♡ **Making requests** ☐
♡ **Saying 'No'** ☐
♡ **Dealing with put-downs** ☐
♡ **Expressing anger** ☐
♡ **Giving criticism** ☐
♡ **Receiving criticism** ☐
And any other situations: ☐

....

Give yourself the opportunity to improve your skills in these areas with application and practice. You will also find helpful information in Anne Dickson's excellent book on assertiveness, *A Woman in Your Own Right.*

Are you still friends with your 'ex'?

In the Agency, we often check out whether a new client is still friends with the 'ex'. If they are, it can be a sign that they can continue to talk through difficult times and are good communicators. It also means that there is less likelihood of unfinished business hanging around to trip them up when they embark on a new relationship.

L♡vebyte

" When I meet a man I ask myself, 'Is this the man I want my children to spend their weekends with? **"**

Rita Rudner

Over-ambitious wish lists

'I'm not settling for Mr Second Best, thank you very much,' is a refrain we hear from every new woman member at the agency. For this, read: 'I'm not going out with any man who isn't drop-dead gorgeous, at the top of his profession AND in touch with his feelings.' In other words they're after a man 'on a pedestal'.

In the 21st century, it's become acceptable to be over-the-top fussy about who your partner is to be. When we get a super-ambitious wish list from an agency applicant, we know that they are unconsciously setting themselves up for failure. Could *you* be doing this with your search for a perfect man? Is this hopeless search for Mr Perfect an unconscious defence against going into a relationship?

When reviewing your partner wish list, keep asking yourself how many attributes you can move from an 'Essentials' list to a 'Desirables' list. Don't turn potential partners down before you've really got to know them as people. 'Nice chap, great for a friend, but no chemistry,' is as likely, if not more than likely, to turn into someone you could love than the love-at-first-sight date. The only way you can really test this is by trying it out – and what can you lose? You probably have to make 10 or more good friendships with men before you have the chance of finding that special relationship. Keep that in mind when you tackle your **Relationship Action Plan** at the end of this chapter.

S☺undbyte

Mr Perfect is the man you've put on a pedestal, but no one can perch on top of a pedestal for long; it always wobbles, the man falls off – and then looks foolish and less fanciable. So, a bit of advice: don't look for Mr Perfect, he really doesn't exist.

The secret, then, is to be prepared to engage with any man who's 'roughly right' and see what you can discover about him. Whatever happens, your preconceptions are bound to be challenged. Check out your friends; you'll find that their partners are rarely more than, say, 60% of what they were seeking in the first place – and the relationship still works out! The next exercise is a neat demonstration of this.

Mansearch Workout – The perfect couples wish-list test

Think of two really happy couples you know and check off the qualities you think the men possess from this typical wish list

	Couple 1	Couple 2
Kind	☐	☐
Sense of humour	☐	☐
In touch with his feelings	☐	☐
Able to talk about feelings	☐	☐
Confident	☐	☐
Ambitious	☐	☐
Works to live, doesn't live to work	☐	☐
Has a challenging job he's passionate about	☐	☐
Well educated	☐	☐
Tall	☐	☐
Looks after himself and is fit	☐	☐
Looks good and has a sense of style	☐	☐
Likes children	☐	☐
Well travelled	☐	☐
Cultured	☐	☐
Within three years of the woman's age	☐	☐

How many did you tick? Seventy % or more and I'll suspect you of cheating; less than this and you can guess that some stuff was dropped from the original wish list of the women in question – and *it doesn't matter*. Wish lists are important, and you can do a preliminary list right now, but I don't recommend putting ticks and crosses on it too early on in a new relationship. *See* Chapter 9, 'How Will I Know When It's Love?', for a further exploration of essential and desirable wish lists.

SMART BIOG: Anthea's Mr Perfect – Raj or Don?

Anthea had known Raj and Don since university. She was cosmopolitan and a lover of adventure. Her career in television and public relations had been dynamic and demanding. And yet she seemed untainted by this – she came across like a breath of fresh air on a spring day; an absolutely delightful person. I met her when I was asked by a glossy magazine to do my 'thing' as a matchmaker for an article they were writing about choosing partners. I had to guess which of two men was her ex-boyfriend and which her fiancé.

First, I asked Anthea all about herself and the kind of man that she had been looking for. 'He's got to have something dangerous and exciting about him,' she told me, 'a little mad, perhaps, and unlikely to be working in a conventional job.' She had studied international relations and was concerned about human-rights issues, so it would be good if he had similar interests. As an after-thought, and with a grin, she mentioned that she was irresistibly attracted to men with stubbly chins! She had given me enough clues. No problem guessing this one, I thought.

I met Raj first. Yes, he did have lovely twinkly eyes and a great sense of humour. He was good looking and terribly nice. But he worked as an accountant and had no sense of danger or adventure about him. He'd scarcely been abroad at all, and liked stay-at-home activities such as watching sport on TV. He hardly ever went to the cinema, let alone the theatre. Don, on the other hand, was also not only handsome but had a certain edge and charisma about him. He'd travelled far and wide and had just spent six months teaching in a poverty-stricken area of Latin America. He came from a cultured, creative family.

I didn't have any doubt: the fiancé must be Don. He was the person she'd described to me. He fitted her shopping list. I'd already married them off, so you could have knocked me down with a feather when I heard from the journalist doing the piece that her fiancé was, in fact, Raj. Don was the 'ex'! And neither had a stubbly chin.

Seeing more than meets the eye

The right man for Anthea was not apparent when she first met him. It took considerable time together as friends before his true attractiveness won her over. She will continue to follow her own interests, as she has always done, and so will he. Anthea has found someone to meet her needs who also allows her to be an individual with her own interests. You may be in danger of passing over many potential men who you think of as wonderful friends but not relationship material. Think again and surprise yourself – as Anthea did. It's all a question of:

♡ Being open minded about meeting likely partners, men who offer possibilities for 'good relating' even though they may be totally different from the ones you've fallen for in the past.

♡ Thinking positive – don't let any lack of characteristics that have attracted you in the past put you off the trail.

The partner who is right for you will appreciate and respect your independence. You don't have to give up the things you value about being single if you've chosen the right man. There are lots of men out there who are right for you, but first you've just got to get up, go out there and meet them. Secondly, you must ensure you're in 'Dating/Flirt Mode' before any spark will ignite – more on this in Chapter 8 on flirting. Last, but not least, you need to ensure your communication skills are honed to enable you sort out and meet each other's needs and respect your differences.

So, now is the time to use the ideas in this chapter to move your partner search forward? Don't just fantasize about it, do something right now! Commit yourself to some actions that will bring about a new perspective and some practical changes in your life. Here are some Prompts to remind you:

Keynotes & Diary Prompts

1 Value being single and the opportunities it offers you to learn about yourself and your needs.
2 Don't make your happiness conditional on going into a relationship.
3 When you go into a relationship, do so as a self-fulfilled individual.
4 Always suspend judgement until you get to know a person.

5 Make a note of communication faults you see in others and ask yourself if you ever behave like this.

6 Check out with friends, family, colleagues what kind of communicator you are. Ask for positives (first) and then recommendations on talking, listening, humour, and giving and receiving criticism, as well as how you come across generally.

7 Do something positive this week to polish your people skills and communication skills. No matter how good you believe they are, make them even better by enrolling on a course or reading a book such as Anne Dickson's *A Woman in Your Own Right.*

RELATIONSHIP ACTION PLAN 2

Note down your Smart Action points for the next week.

Positive Action 1:

....

....

Positive Action 2:

....

....

Positive Action 3:

....

....

Treats

TREAT yourself well and others will too. You deserve it, especially if you stick to your plan. Get out your Diary now (have you found that beautiful notebook yet?) and schedule something special for you – and just for you – every single day. What's it to be today?

♡ If you're still very post-work hyper, *put on some good dance music* while you tidy up or make your supper – or just dance!

♡ If you're absolutely exhausted, how about a *relaxing bath before supper* – a few drops of lavender is always very soothing. For a delicious after-a-hard-day mixture, combine your drops of lavender with drops of rose geranium.

♡ Make a note in your diary to *book yourself a massage – or a series of massages!*

When it came to men, Maya could never resist a challenge.

chapter 3

Dating Secrets of Smart Women

Meeting men – why leave it to chance?

You are an independent woman but, like all human beings, you have a need
for intimacy, and an intimate relationship is maybe the best way for you to feel
really fulfilled. However, it is all very well theorizing about how to make first
dates and relationships work, but what if there is no one to have a relationship
with? As we saw in Chapter 1, for some women the opportunities hardly seem to
exist for meeting available, single men of a similar outlook and background –
or do they?

It is always a source of amazement, to those of us working at my introduction agencies, that well-organized and businesslike people behave quite
out of character when faced with the need to find a mate. If you were seeking a new employee to fill the most important post in your company, the
likelihood is that you'd appoint a specialist recruitment agency to headhunt
appropriate candidates and/or you'd advertise and network like crazy. You
wouldn't wait for a qualified person to turn up just by accident. The same is
true if you were hoping to buy a new house – the chances of stumbling upon
the home of your dreams without employing an estate agent or, at the very
least, looking at the property ads, are very slight indeed. However, for some
unfathomable reason, when it comes to relationships it is all meant to happen
by magic.

L♡vebyte

❝ Dreaming is the poor retreat of the lazy, hopeless and imperfect lover. **❞**
William Congreve, *Love for Love* (1695)

Those smart women who are 'in the know' use all possible opportunities to extend their network of contacts. This way they will meet a much larger range of potential partners. If you're not meeting new people in the first place, then you're colluding with failure – and this is your choice. Remember that *you* are in charge, and nothing will change unless *you make it*. Set yourself goals for meeting suitable men: aim for, say, a new one every month for the next six months. This should certainly get you back into practice.

Below are a number of ways you can try to meet men. You don't, of course, need to try all of my suggestions; you may well find some of the first ideas far too forward and cheeky for your nature (those towards the end of the Chapter are the easier options); but – nothing ventured, nothing gained. Chapter 4 offers meeting-men suggestions that require less bravado, but mug up on these cheeky options first – you never know when you may need them!

A word of warning, here; although I'm advocating being really businesslike about creating dating networks and opportunities, once you're *on* that first date *forget all about it*. The women who 'interview' their date to see if he measures up to the 'job spec'? – well, this spells disaster. This is the time to ditch the strategic businesswoman and tune into feeling fantastically flirty, having great fun and simply discovering another human being.

Never walk alone on the wild side
Needless to say, any ultra-cheeky approach needs to go hand-in-hand with an ultra-careful attitude to personal safety. NEVER let a man have your address or terrestrial phone number until you are absolutely sure you can trust him, and you should NEVER be with strangers except in a safe, public context.

Be cheeky!

Smart women are always ready to grab the unexpected opportunity. It used to be only men who seized chances for a chat-up line or played metaphorical footsy. Now, women are in a strong enough position to do so with stylish aplomb. Every glossy magazine has run a piece on how to pick up Mr Wonderful when you spot him. One British magazine, *Time Out*, even has an adverts column called 'Once Seen' for those who've missed their chance and vainly hope to recapture the moment when, if only they'd been forward enough, they could have met the love of their life instead of their eyes just meeting across a crowded room. So, imagination to the fore! Be ready to seize the moment. Here are some opportunities to look out for.

Electronic triggers

An electronic trigger is not one of those Japanese dating bleepers that light up when someone compatible comes within range. This is any other electronic gadget with male appeal – preferably just on the market, genuinely useful *and* which will work a treat for getting into a conversation with a man you've strategically sat near on a train, a plane or in a café. When Palm Pilot electronic organizers first came out (light years ago) I would often use mine with a full-size but fold-away keyboard and start word-processing on it while I was drinking my cappuccino in a cafe – and well, wow! A man invariably came along and asked me all about it – you know how they love gadgets. (Knowing my penchant for writing this book in cafés, my staff gave me a Palm keyboard for a Christmas present.) Any unusual electronic gadgetry will have the same effect. In fact, anything techie that will give men an excuse to start chatting.

At the supermarket – yes, really!

The supermarket is definitely an OK place for a female to loiter safely and take time to select whom she wants to bump into. Our up-front woman might be heard to utter 'Have you the remotest idea how to cook this?' as she picks up some alien vegetable within earshot of a suitable man. Otherwise, of course, you can simply fling all your shopping into his trolley when he's caught up in choosing a ripe melon, discovering a minute later what a fool you've been to have thought his trolley was *yours*. In the ensuing mayhem you can decide whether it's worth taking things further. If you're a bit crazy, then this one is well worth trying. It works – I know; I've done it – 'accidentally', of course.

L♡vebyte

" A girl never pursues a man; but then a mousetrap never pursues a mouse. **"**
Ronnie Barker

Art galleries – for old masters and new mistresses

Another safe place for women to hang about in, and much more selective than the supermarket, is the art gallery. Don't buy a catalogue just ask to take a peep at the one that belongs to the particular man on whom you have focused your curiosity while he is absorbed in studying some challenging creation. For instance, the Victoria and Albert Museum in London claims many romantic successes at its lecture evenings targeted at singles. Check out what's available near you. Get yourself invited to private views, especially at smaller, more interesting galleries where the wine on offer facilitates mixing and mingling. *Don't pretend you know more than you do:* you'll come across as pompous and ignorant and regret it deeply. Try and ask intelligent questions – a great flirt tactic.

SMART BIOG: Selina nearly fails to meet her match

Selina, a 26-year-old fashion stylist, had a friend doing a postgraduate course in Fine Art at London University. One day, when she was really overwhelmed with work, she received an invitation to a gallery opening where the friend had some paintings in an exhibition. She meant to ring him to say she was busy, but forgot. Feeling it would be unkind not to attend, as it was a big moment for the friend, she reluctantly dragged herself along. A glass of wine and some stimulating conversation about the exhibits ended up with a group going off for a Chinese meal together with the gallery owner, Sean. A month later Selina and Sean were an item. Six months later they were engaged.

If music be the food of love – try concerts

Like art galleries, concerts are selective, and at least you know that you'll enjoy the same kind of music as the men attending. At classical concerts, the 'Please could I have a quick look at your programme' technique works well. During the performance itself, see if you can spot an empty seat next to an unaccompanied man and discreetly slip into it during the interval, asking if it's taken and remarking on how much better you'll enjoy the sound from your improved vantage point. Your mutual appreciation (or otherwise) of the music should do the rest!

SMART BIOG: Mara finds him underground

Every morning on her way to work in the underground Mara couldn't help but notice an intriguing man who always took the same corner seat and got off after she did. He was of medium height with black curly hair and a shy smile; not exactly good-looking, but with a quiet energy which she found attractive. Mara liked the way he dressed – he seemed to have a strong line in colourful shirts. Was she imagining it or did his eyes appear to linger on her longer than the other passengers? She noticed that he even read the same newspaper as she did. She fantasized about an accidental meeting where they got chatting and he invited her out on a date but, needless to say, there was no invitation – at least, not till she made it happen.

One morning, Mara took a deep breath and smiling nervously handed him a note as she got off the train. It said 'I'd love to chat with you – do give me a ring', followed by her name and mobile number. Well, his name was Alex and he did ring her that very evening. They chatted for ages and discovered a lot about one another, including the fact that Alex was eight years younger than Mara.

They went on one date together and found that they had nothing much in common, apart from the same underground line; so, with a warm hug, they wished each other well and parted company. Mara and Alex still see one another on the train and always say 'Hi'. Although nothing came of the relationship, the fact that Mara had taken the initiative – and hadn't been struck down by lightning as a result – was an enormous breakthrough. Her blossoming spirit of adventure prompted her to join **Drawing Down the Moon** and this is how she met her husband Stuart. They then proceeded to break all the agency rules – their first date lasted 22 hours, they became engaged a week later and were married within a few months! Take a risk! Go for it! One situation triggers another. It's **Domino Dating** again!

L♡vebyte

" A bachelor never quite gets over the idea that he is a thing of beauty and a joy forever. **"**
Helen Rowland, *A Guide to Married Men*

Scoring in the street
Approach the man you fancy. You're lost (again). (Make it strategically plausible!) He is outside the train station or at a bus stop or buying a newspaper. You need directions to somewhere in (what just happens to be) the same area that he might be heading – not far away. He may even be tempted to accompany you there but of course you'll only let him if the venue is a public one such as a cafe – safety first.

Sign up your local talent
If you feel you're even mildly political, or just a sociable animal, consider becoming more active in your local residents' association or pressure group. Going from house to house, getting signatures for a petition against the building of the new car park or whatever, is an excellent way of meeting people and

striking up new friendships. One of my neighbours gives a party every year for all the residents in our bit of the street. Try this yourself. You'll be very popular and have a lot of fun watching people with totally different interests get on like a house on fire. Who knows, you might find, as I did myself, that the man of your dreams lives right next door. Keep up with local papers and internet sites for details of what is going on in your neck of the woods.

Men with sweat appeal: try aviation sports – or start to train!
Do your research thoroughly here, as some activities attract more men than others. Paragliding and aviation sports are male dominated – but costly, and require some degree of bravery. My first paragliding attempt landed me in a tree, and I wasn't even looking for a man. Sub-aqua is brilliant for men, as many of the women I know can testify.

On the subject of physical activity, I'm told by lots of my introduction agency members (who all *claim* that they attend at least twice a week) that the gym is a rotten place to meet your future partner. I think that all that sweat and those rippling biceps may be the problem. However, a friend of mine, who is a personal trainer to the rich and famous, asserts the opposite: that many of the members of the gym in which she works *do* pair off. It depends on whether you have an imaginative approach. Remember that they are not necessarily all muscle-bound fanatics. You might need help with weightlifting technique or on how to use a machine. The permutations of equipment and movements allow strategic positioning and also enable you to show off your good physical attributes.

L♡vebyte

66 I think the only good thing to be said about leotards is that they're a very effective deterrent against any sort of unwanted sexual attention. If you're wearing stretch knickers, and stretch tights, and a stretch leotard, you might as well try and sexually harass a trampoline. 99
Victoria Wood

Wine tasting
Wine tasting is a real winner. You don't have to be a seasoned wine connoisseur. Many more women are excelling themselves as experts in this field, but it's still very much a man's province. Women 'in the know' keep secret the fact that one can meet very interesting and classy single men on wine-tasting courses. You won't need any tips about how to get chatting – the wine will look after that, unless you're super-correct and spit it all out (what a waste!).

Shop around carefully. Christie's and Sotheby's, the upmarket auctioneers in London, run excellent but pricey courses. Look out, also, for courses run by the Wine Education Council – great value. The more budget-minded might investigate their local adult-education centre.

Shopping for designer ties – you'll need help

You say to the man you've got your eye on, 'I just can't make up my mind about which of these two ties I should buy for my brother. Please, do tell me which you think is the nicest.' The only problem with this one is that you may end up buying a lot of ties. So, thank him for the advice, following through with your chat line of course, then say you are going to look in another shop before you make up your mind about the tie – and, Oh! 'What about a cup of coffee?'

Catch him at cookery class

Whether run by your local adult-education centre or some posh cookery school, a cookery class is a superb pick-up point! OK, so there are lots of women there too, but the men who attend are often looking for a partner and are more than willing to flirt over the finer points of making risotto al funghi or Thai chicken with lemon grass. There are so many opportunities for getting into conversation or setting up an informal get-together afterwards! Great fun, and you can certainly make some new friends.

L♡vebyte

❝ A woman who thinks the way to a man's heart is through his stomach is aiming a little too high. ❞
Anon

Adult-education classes

I used to run an adult-education centre and while I know it is true that classes are, in general, female dominated, men do attend. We used to let people visit, or 'sit in', on a class so they could see if it was what they wanted or at the right level. Ask if you can do this – and then you can check out the man-search rating of classes without committing yourself. This is a sensible move because stereotypically male-dominated subjects (such as woodwork) may turn out to be attended mostly by women.

Modern teaching styles stress student interaction, so it's relatively easy to get to know your class-mates. Your common interest in the subject will mean no problems in starting a conversation in the tea break. Drinks in the local bar or pub afterwards are easy to suggest. Whether or not you meet Mr Wonderful, you should have a great time acquiring a new interest – whether it's fluency in Italian or a facility with spreadsheets.

S⦿undbyte – The offer they can't refuse

When you're interested in furthering 'togetherness' after a class or some other activity, avoid saying, 'Would you like to join us for a drinks session after the class?' Instead, say, 'You're invited to join us for a drink ... coming?' A positive personal invitation is hard to refuse.

Dancing

Whether your taste is ceroc, salsa or even tango, dancing is a great way to meet men. If you've got two left feet (like me) and need a bit of guidance, check out classes in local clubs, gyms and adult-education centres. Even book a couple of private tuition sessions beforehand if you're scared of making a fool of yourself – I did this for some Salsa and it was wonderful for dispelling nerves and building confidence.

Dancing is also a wonderful way of working off tension, dispelling depression and keeping fit. You'll need no tips on getting into conversation and you'll be a wow at parties.

Holidays

The problem with many holidays specifically for singles is that, unless you have chosen one of the companies that promises equal numbers, more women than men will usually have booked in. Make some careful checks in advance: the male/female ratio, age balance, shared background, communal interests – are they right for you? Adventure and special-interest holidays attract a lot of single people.

There is a wide range of organizations that provide packages for single people; personal recommendation is the best way to find one that is likely to suit you – so ask around among your friends.

If you're a friendly person and able to socialize easily with strangers, much the best plan is to avoid package holidays and simply make your own arrangements. A woman travelling alone will always make friends, and there are so many excuses to get talking when you are by yourself.

Travelling with a group of friends feels good – but it is almost always a cop out because you will most probably stay within the confines of the group and avoid the bother of striking up acquaintances with other people. Travelling with friends does, of course, get round the feeling of being alone – but do make the extra effort to go off by yourself for (at least) a day to give yourself the chance of meeting new people.

Borrow a dog

'Can my dog say hello to your dog?' as an opening line never fails. No dog? Borrow a stylish or characterful hound from a lazy friend – just say you need the exercise.

Work – better not!

Most of my agency members tell me that it's unwise, or even out of the question, to have a relationship with a colleague at work. Yet, although most high-powered companies frown on workplace dalliances, a lot of people do still meet this way. If you work in a single-sex environment, or with people from a widely differing age group or social background, then it's likely to be a non-starter.

The competitive nature of most working environments means that it is difficult to flirt because the atmosphere isn't relaxed. You are also opening yourself up to the accusation that you only got your promotion because you slept with your date. Worse still, you could be accused of sexual harassment.

After the convention/seminar – relaxing over dinner ...

Although it's unwise to consider a workplace romance, there is another way to exploit the work dimension. Professional seminars and conventions are rich hunting grounds. Some people tell me that they don't want to meet another solicitor, doctor or whatever; but if this is your view, think again. Your common interests will keep the conversation lively from the start – and throughout any relationship that develops. Also, you'll understand each other's work pressures and be able to offer mutual support during tricky times. Such a meeting place is, therefore, not such a bad idea. Get yourself on the appropriate mailing lists. Head for events that have social time programmed in – such as meals, drinks, entertainment and workshops.

Talent at the DIY store

I have it on very good authority that you can nail your man in DIY stores with a technical question on the use of paint products, hammer drills or flat-pack cupboards. The male-dominated customer base is just waiting to be asked for its expertise! Poor staffing levels ensure you have a great excuse to require advice from a fellow customer. There's bound to be a store near you.

L♡vebyte

❝ Whenever you want to marry someone, go have lunch with his ex-wife. **❞**
Shelley Winters

Your ready-made sales team – your friends

There is another opportunity that already exists for you, but which might need a bit of tweaking – your friendship network. It's no bad thing to own up to wanting a relationship. Indeed, if you do, you'll find that most of your friends will secretly admire you. Be absolutely up front and offer an irresistible prize to the one who introduces you to your future life partner – a new car or a fantastic holiday, if you can afford it. More realistically, what about knitting a fabulous sweater or painting their bedroom? It will be cheap at the price.

Everyone loves to be a matchmaker, and who better than someone who knows you really well. Friends *do* know of single men but they just haven't thought of introducing them to you. Perhaps they secretly think you're too fussy. If you have already enlisted the support of a **Dating Buddy**, ensure that he or she is *really* keeping their eyes open for likely opportunities; remind them when you do your weekly feedback call.

Get yourself invited to as many parties as possible through friends. I know parties are hard work; walking into a room full of people is always a bit scary. My own survival tip, when there's no one to introduce you, is don't try to break into conversation with two people standing together – you may feel the 'odd one out'. Instead, head for men standing on their own or in groups of three or more, with or without women. What do you say? Variations on, 'Hello; can I join you? I'm Susan,' are simple and always seem to do the job. This can be followed by, 'Don't let me interrupt the conversation – what were you talking about?'

Singles' parties

If you can't face being so brazen, why not throw a party for a bunch of friends and ask each guest to bring a single unattached man with them – they can't come unless they do. If nothing else, your reputation as a hostess will soar.

Mansearch opportunity ratings

Now for the next Workout. This is your opportunity to review all the opportunities you have at present for meeting interesting, available men. It is good to have an overview of what is available, then you can expand on it.

Mansearch Workout – Opportunities for meeting men

Rate each of the following Mansearch Opportunities within your reach. Tick 0–5 depending on how likely they are to yield possible encounters for you. Don't rule anything out yet just because you haven't the nerve to use it. That's for later.

	Rating					
Work	0	1	2	3	4	5
Friends	0	1	2	3	4	5
Family	0	1	2	3	4	5
Neighbourhood	0	1	2	3	4	5
Sports and exercise	0	1	2	3	4	5
Education	0	1	2	3	4	5
Holidays	0	1	2	3	4	5
Clubs	0	1	2	3	4	5
Supermarkets	0	1	2	3	4	5
Art galleries	0	1	2	3	4	5
Concerts	0	1	2	3	4	5
Others (name them):						
....	0	1	2	3	4	5
....	0	1	2	3	4	5
....	0	1	2	3	4	5

Go a little crazy. This exercise is to loosen you up a bit!

'How contrived – to try and organize something as ephemeral as romance!', you're maybe saying grumpily to yourself as you read this chapter. Just remember that in the old days, this matchmaking business was carried out by the extended family and the local community. Without these institutions working for you today, either you have to take the matter into your own hands or employ professionals to undertake it for you – so, for the moment, continue to examine do-it-yourself possibilities. Once you've identified your range of opportunities and rated them, move on to the next Mansearch Workout.

Mansearch Workout – My most likely opportunities for DIY matchmaking

From all the opportunities you found in the last Workout, choose those which have a rating of three or more and make your shortlist.

1) ....

2) ....

3) ....

4) ....

5) ....

You should now have at least three new ideas for action. Enter your new list in your diary with a deadline of, say, two weeks to get moving. Do remember that, the older you are, the fewer possibilities there are to meet a partner – so you'll have to work all the harder to create them.

If you need encouragement, invite your Dating Buddy, or anyone of the get-up-and-go variety, to accompany you to the wine tasting or the ceroc class. Once you are there, let go of the task in hand and simply enjoy yourself. That way, developments are likely to be more spontaneous.

What do you say after you say 'hello'?

How can you capture his interest sufficiently in that quick 'spontaneous' encounter you've taken such trouble to plan? It's not so much what you say as how you say it. Skip briefly to Chapter 8 and sample some flirty ways you can open a conversation with a stranger. It's all about acquiring the technique for getting yourself into a happy, relaxed, anything-goes emotional state and using practice to build confidence. Try the techniques suggested often and you'll soon become fluent at friendly and fascinating flirtation.

Body language speaks volumes. What does yours say about you? Check out Allan Pease's book, *Body Language - How to Read Others' Thoughts by Their Gestures.*

'I'd rather march naked down the street than pick up a stranger!'

Of course, I've guessed that some of you will say that the whole business of approaching strangers is too stressful. If that's your position, you need to move rapidly on to the next chapter (Chapter 4, 'Agencies, Ads and Action') and think about roping in professional help – as you would with any other aspect of your life. The amazing thing is that, once you start meeting attractive new people (however you organize it) exciting new possibilities tend to open up on all fronts. Why? You're more relaxed about the whole business – and this makes you more attractive. We notice this every day in the introduction business.

Keynotes & Diary Prompts

1 Review your list of existing Mansearch Opportunities: how/where to encounter single men in an atmosphere conducive to a bit of light flirtation.
2 Discuss this list with someone supportive, maybe with your Dating Buddy.
3 Enter in your Diary the deadline dates for implementing your Smart Dating Plan and then make it happen.
4 Safety first. Always meet in a public place and have your own transport home.

RELATIONSHIP ACTION PLAN 3

Note down your Smart Action points for the next week:

Positive Action 1:

....

....

Positive Action 2:

....

....

Positive Action 3:

....

....

Treats

What's it to be today? Before you read Chapter 4, do something deservedly self-spoiling to make you feel on top of the world:

♡ *Buy yourself a bunch of flowers* on the way home from work (making sure their colour is really 'singing to your heart').

♡ Fortified by a glass of good wine – or a cup of cinnamon and mango tea, *open your wardrobe and throw out at least three things* that do nothing for you – ignoring such 'facts' as:

a) they cost a lot; and b) there's nothing wrong with them. You're making way for the new!

♡ Arrange with friend(s) to go on an *out-of-neighbourhood outing* – picnic by the river, drive to nearby countryside for walk, visit a stately home.

How would Kate recognize her blind date? Paul told her his colleagues frequently remarked on his resemblance to Keanu Reeves.

chapter 4

Agencies, Ads, the Internet and Action

Learn music from musicians and dating from ...

Do any of these scenarios sound familiar?

♡ You are busy – your professional life as a marketing director is sending you all over the world. You usually sleep on the plane – and miss the opportunity to ask your attractive neighbour if you can borrow his magazine ...

♡ You seem endlessly to be on night duty or on call at the hospital. Parties and nightclubs have become a thing of the past.

♡ Approaching men for help when 'lost' in the metro or unsure about drill-bit sizes at the DIY warehouse is a hopeless dream. The kids would be standing beside you – gawping.

Well, clearly you are going to have to find another way. Fortunately there are plenty of them. What's more, there are lots of people in a position similar to yours, and they are exploring these ways, too.

The main choices on the menu are the off-line personal dating agencies, internet dating, dining clubs, speed dating, singles events and voice personals. A number of services now have both off-line and on-line elements and the boundaries between the two are beginning to blur. In this chapter I'll concentrate mainly on the off-line possibilities as now that internet dating has become so popular I have given it the next chapter all to itself.

These exciting new dating options are 21st-century replacements for the extended family, the local community and the dances and tennis parties that used to facilitate suitable matches in earlier generations. Plug yourself in to some of these new circuits. They can enable you to compress a lifetime of dating opportunities into as little as six months. Various people you know are probably doing it already; they're just keeping the good news to themselves. If you were searching for a new job, or buying a house, you would ask for your friends' advice, look at ads, seek out agents to put you in touch, and so on – so why not use similar strategies when seeking Mr Right?

There are so many ways to meet nowadays if you decide to be proactive and adventurous. My Domino Dating Strategy suggests that you'll find your future love more quickly if you go for volume and use several different dating solutions at the same time. But remember that if you meet someone special and start to explore a serious relationship do stop meeting other people.

Introduction agencies – bring in the professionals!

If there are few chances of meeting available men in your own environment, then it's a great idea to go to the people who *have* got the contacts. Some people may still feel reticent about using introduction agencies, but nowadays they have shaken off the rather tawdry, losers' image they had in the middle of the last century. Indeed, you'll find that the type of person who uses good agencies is more positive and successfully assertive than the norm. At the **Drawing Down the Moon** we wouldn't dream of inviting anyone to join unless they had a good relationship history and social skills. After all, if they lack the ability to make relationships, it's unlikely they will click with any of our existing members.

However, in my view, personal introduction agencies don't work equally well for everyone. They are probably the best choice for women between 22 and 55, and men between 27 and about 60. Outside these age groups, most introduction agencies usually cannot provide the necessary volume of potential partners. The exception to this can be if the agency in question is prepared to undertake a bespoke, headhunting mission for you as Drawing Down the Moon does. Always check out the proportion of suitable men that an agency has available for you to meet. Don't forget the customary age gap between men and women which skews the statistics. You may disapprove of it but don't let the issue distract you from your search for a lovely man.

If you are a woman over 40, remember that you are likely to be competing with younger women for the same men. It may take you longer to reach the minimum number of introductions that agencies normally guarantee. But the man you are searching for may just be waiting for you right now on an agency database. I always say that there are enough men somewhere out there for women in any age group – as long as the women are pro-active. Furthermore, my **Domino Dating Strategy** works – so go for two or more different dating options.

Keen to have babies? Don't be so keen that you insist on "only meeting men who want children". You will rule out the majority of men who feel they can't agree to this definitely until they have explored a potential relationship over a period of time. If you tell the agency that you won't meet men who haven't explicitly said they want babies, you will hardly meet anyone. Quite reasonably, men are worried about meeting a woman who is, first and foremost, looking for a stud.

Remember, Domino Dating? Meet as many lovely guys as possible and don't try and pin any of them down on the baby issue right away – it is a major saboteur for late thirties women seeking a relationship. Most of our couples who end up having kids together will own that if "babies" had been a precondition of dating, they would never have met.

L♡vebyte

❝ Thirty-five is a very attractive age: London society is full of women who have of their own free choice remained thirty-five for years. ❞
Oscar Wilde

Finding the good introduction agency

I am often asked for advice on choosing an agency. It is amazing how few people keep their wits about them when doing this. If they were searching for any other service, such as a personal trainer or a builder, they would shop around and ask their friends for recommendations. Because a lot of agency-users keep their membership a secret, you may think yourself the only person you know who has ever contemplated joining one, so it may not occur to you to consult your friends. If you did, you might get a surprise! Without proper advice, too many people simply opt for the first agency that sends them a brochure or they find on Google without evaluating what's on offer.

My main recommendation is to check that the agency is a member of the established trade association that is working hard to improve the standards of the industry. I'm not saying that every agency which is not a member is unsatisfactory, but I would be wary of those that aren't. The Association of British

Introduction Agencies (ABIA) has been around for over twenty five years and has around 30 members – www.abia.org.uk.

Spotting the quick-buck merchants

Sometimes people set up agencies without adequate preparation and resources in the hope of making easy money. For a new agency, the first couple of years are always a challenge. It takes time to build up membership and accumulate enough people to provide appropriate introductions. Some claim many years in business, but their previous operating sites may have been abroad and they may be new to your country. Other agencies offer free membership to the first couple of hundred members as a way around the problem of 'starter' numbers. They may, however, underestimate the cost of servicing their 'free' members (before they are in a position to take money from paying clients) and end up out of business. So, here are a few tips:

♡   Always choose an agency that has been around for at least two years.

♡   Watch out for agencies that won't give their prices up front.

♡   If you are in a difficult-to-match age group, beware of those agencies that assure you they have plenty of people for you to meet.

♡   Avoid those agencies using high-pressure sales techniques.

L♡vebyte

" *Man:* So, wanna go back to my place?
Woman: Well, I don't know. Will two people fit under a rock? **"**

The personal introduction agency

Most personal dating agencies interview their members before inviting them to join. They sort the wheat from the chaff and can save you an enormous amount of time – which is immensely valuable for busy professionals. Some only interview after the fee has been paid and in these cases it's possible that the screening could be less rigorous. They offer a variety of matching procedures, some allowing you to choose your own potential partner, others choosing for you. Some use photos and some don't. You can often learn a lot about the background and lifestyle of the people concerned, and what their interests are in a good personal agency.

How we do it at Drawing Down the Moon

At Drawing Down the Moon in addition to the usual background information, we ask about what films and plays you may have seen lately, what your favourite music is, what you'd do in an ideal day and much else. These culture and life-style questions help to paint a more intelligent portrait of the individual and give insight into their values and outlook. All of this is essential for a good match.

A limited number of members subscribe to the option of choosing their own potential partners from profiles and photos. But interestingly, we find that we get more happy endings when the matchmakers do the choosing! When we are trying to match someone we usually have several members of the team on the case, each contributing their personal knowledge about the individuals concerned.

Feedback after dates is a vital part of the Drawing Down the Moon system. This is given on the phone, in person to the matchmakers or members can use our confidential intranet. This is enormously helpful for considering future matches. We never give feedback directly to the member it concerns without the per-mission of the originating party. It is more constructive and tactful to only proffer feedback in general terms on request when we would offer suggestions about how it can be handled. This gives the Drawing Down the Moon system a big plus over "real life" outside where one rarely has the opportunity to learn what other people really think about you.

Drawing Down the Moon also offers a 'VIP' membership for those wanting a truly made-to-measure, headhunting service. We call this the 'Personal Matchmaker Option'. The search for a really good match is carried out, not only amongst the Agency membership but also further afield. Sometimes they could be cherry picked from a niche internet dating site or one of our "dating ambassadors" may tap a potential match on the shoulder at a conference or social event.

I met a great guy in the check-in queue at the airport a couple of months ago – he was handsome, very well educated, successful, a great listener and best of all, had very twinkly eyes. "Never let a good man go to waste" I thought as I did a ten minute, on-the-spot "pre-interview" as discreetly as I could and took his card with a view to booking him in with us. He was happily introduced to a prospec-tive match we were headhunting for within a week or so. Fingers crossed! And last week I encountered a really fab guy through Freecycle.com when I was off-loading some vintage film equipment I'd been hoarding for years. Over a glass of

wine in my kitchen I discovered that he was a successful TV director in his forties, recently single and now ready to move on. Well, I couldn't wait to get him
to meet Kate, my senior interviewer, as I knew she was headhunting for a particular woman he would be ideal for. It's these sort of encounters YOU should be
looking out for – and don't be backward in coming forward!

We also work with other dating agencies who will do a specific search for us
on an occasional basis. All such prospective dates are interviewed and ID
checked by us just the same as regular Agency applicants and only if they are
up to scratch we will introduce them. Every prospective match for a Personal
Matchmaker member is first discussed with both parties. It's a lot of work for
us matchmakers but results indicate a really high hit rate! It's a way of com-
bining the volume of the world outside with the internet and the selective
approach of a personal agency.

There are lots of personal introduction agencies to choose from, so do shop
around. Ask them the right questions and you should find one that suits you.
Do bear in mind that the more selective a personal introduction agency is, the
higher the fees because overheads are greater. They have to fund the heavy
costs of the advertising needed to recruit the right type of people for you to
meet. Also, they often operate from expensive, centrally-located offices so
they are accessible to more potential clients and they have to support a greater
staff-to-member ratio than non-personal agencies.

S⚙undbyte

Remember that if you continue to take no action, nothing in your life is likely to
change much. If, on the other hand, you explore new possibilities, even if you don't
immediately meet Mr Right, you will at least have got yourself into dating mode –
an important first step in achieving the Domino Dating Effect.

The niche agency

Niche agencies target a specific minority group – religious, ethnic or interest
related. They can be personal agencies, computer, list-method or voice-mail
agencies. Those I've come across include ones especially for plump people, veg-
etarians, gays, people of Asian origin, Jewish groups, the physically challenged
and those interested in classical music. The problem here is self-exclusion. Few
of us like to define ourselves only by one trait or activity. By narrowing down

the field, you may miss many other opportunities but, for some people with very specific requirements, these agencies may be ideal. Niche dating agencies can be on-line or off-line.

How to handle agencies and get the answers you want

When considering an agency, ask for an interview if it's off-line and go armed with lots of questions. Obviously, the less expensive agencies don't normally give interviews as their business is conducted by post, phone or internet, but see what information you can glean to put you more in the picture. The sort of questions you should be asking are:

Compatible geography
Find out how many potential partners live in your area. A national agency may have only a few people near your home. If you have to travel miles to meet dates, then a relationship has little chance of getting off the ground. However, if you live in a remote district, you will have to be prepared to put more effort into travelling.

Ratio of men to women
Many agencies imply that they have equal numbers of men and women when what they really mean is that they have more younger men and more older women. This problem has been caused by rises and falls in the birth rate combined with the fact that more women tend to pair off with older men. Even if you are an older woman who prefers younger men, they may be reluctant to meet you! You have to be very realistic about this, whatever your views about the rights and wrongs of the situation.

Members' backgrounds
Does the agency have members who are likely to be compatible with you? Even if you'd personally prefer a classless society, you'll find that a similar social class background is one of the main determinants of success in a relationship. This isn't saying that people from one class are better or more interesting than those from another; it's simply about people being able to share the same experiences and values, about being able to laugh at the same jokes and aspire to similar lifestyles. It is very difficult to cross class and cultural boundaries in close relationships. Friendship is different: we can encompass many different kinds of people when we don't actually have to live with them.

Another important point to remember is that, in today's multi-ethnic societies, someone's ethnic origin may or may not tell you much about their culture. It is highly probable that a second or third-generation black or Asian person could have everything in common with someone from the similar educational and social background but whose skin colour and ethnic origin happen to be white. Check out your pre-conceptions before jumping to conclusions.

L♡vebyte

" A different taste in jokes is a great strain on the affections. **"**
   George Eliot, *'Daniel Deronda'* (1876)

Agencies' staff ratios
When off-line dating agencies are first launched, they usually have enough staff to recruit members. However, they don't always allow for the fact that they will need extra personnel once they are up and running. Some agencies skimp on this aspect of their organization. Should it be a personal agency, it is also worth asking if the consultant who initially interviews you will be the same one who actually does the matching. If this isn't the case, ask them to read back to you the briefing profile to be given to the matchmakers.

Where do the agencies advertise?
Do these agencies advertise in media you approve of and are likely to read yourself? Quite often the newspaper or magazine you choose says quite a bit about your values and outlook. Beware of any agencies that advertise in pornographic magazines – you can surreptitiously check out the top shelves in your local newsagent.

However, I should point out that the internet is where you will now find most introduction agency adverts as offline advertising is proving less effective for them. Check out Google, Yahoo or your favourite search engine. If computers and the internet still present a challenge for you, do drop in at your local library where you can usually have access to these plus some help with getting started.

An introduction agency or dating site will multiply your dating opportunities. Remember, however, that joining one will not necessarily result in a happy ending. Everything that happens in real life also happens in introduction agencies and on line. You can experience rejection and disappointment as well as the excitement and buzz of meeting someone very special. Introduction agencies and dating sites are tools not a panacea.

SMART BIOG: Claudia uses the selective approach to find her Frenchman

Claudia was a 36-year-old economic-development consultant. After being single for about three years with zero dating possibilities on the horizon she decided to give introduction agencies a whirl. She signed up for one where members were interviewed in their own home. Excellent, she thought, the agency will have a very good idea of the kind of men she should be matched with. Seeing a man in his own habitat would give the interviewer a much deeper insight into life style and values. However, although she dated about 12 men in the right age group and location, somehow they seemed very different from her in their ambitions and way of life. Although they were professional and reasonably well educated, none of them were as well travelled and cosmopolitan (Claudia spoke four languages – the result of being a diplomat's daughter). At first she thought that this shouldn't matter and really tried to be open to a relationship developing. The problem was that the men she met, who were all very nice but fairly parochial in outlook, were all fish out of water when they met her friends. She spoke to the agency and found that the notes they held on their computer didn't take into account the fact that Claudia wanted a man who was erudite, cultured, well travelled and multilingual. Also she discovered that people were only interviewed *after* they had paid and virtually no one was turned away as being unsuitable. In other words, the system wasn't selective enough for her particular needs. For others who are perhaps less demanding, she heard it worked really well.

If Claudia had done her homework properly she would have realized the agency's shortcomings and saved precious time as well as money. She came to see us at Drawing Down the Moon and was impressed that no one was invited to join until they had been interviewed and their matchability within our system assessed.

The delightful twist to the story is that we found Claudia's Mr Right, a charming Parisian, now living in London, called Jean-Pierre, and guess what – he turned out to be a close friend of her friend Ross who had no idea that she was interested in finding a partner. Ross had always imagined that Claudia had an army of men in pursuit because she was so attractive. To make amends for his lack of awareness, he was best man at their wedding. Remember, friends often need reminding that they can and should play Cupid.

Other dating organizations

Dining clubs

There are many different types of dining club, and they are certainly an excellent way to make new friends of either sex. The standard format is tables organized according to loose age-groupings. The seating will be organized for you on the basis of man/woman, man/woman. Usually, there is some arrangement to change places once or twice between courses which often leads to friendly mayhem and increases your exposure to new potential dates.

Dining clubs aren't cheap, often at least double the cost of the meal, and most of them use quite up-market restaurants. Before you reel in horror at the price, remember the overheads – advertising and recruiting participants, organizing dates, bookings and seating. I used to run dinner parties and we had a desperate time finding enough men to balance the women in the over-35 group. There was always someone who cancelled at the last moment, leaving us frantically trying to fill an empty seat next to a guest expecting to meet someone fascinating. Fortunately, after much tearing out of hair, we always did manage to find an excellent replacement – and many successful matches resulted.

Some people say that the atmosphere around the dining table can get competitive if more than one person fancies the same man (or woman). Others find it a relaxed way to make new friends of either sex – and it can be great fun along the way!

Singles' social evenings

These social evenings are regular get-togethers of more or less equal numbers of single men and women at a fashionable bar with staff acting as icebreakers. 'The Single Solution' in London is very good. You can view details on line of the singles already signed up and check out if they're your type or not before you register yourself. They tend to be predominantly professionals (see www.thesinglesolution.co.uk). Another excellent organisation is Meet at Last which runs events are for unattached people who enjoy meeting in a relaxed atmosphere where they can mingle, chat, enjoy a couple of drinks, dance, eat, whatever (see *www.meetatlast.com*).

Speed dating – flirting in the fast lane

If the idea of speed dating sounds to you like just a gimmick, you're wrong. In fact, speed dating works wonderfully. No one can avoid being relaxed and gregarious in the hilarity that results from these fun evenings. Be under no illusion that you can *really* get to know anyone properly via these encounters. They are simply a useful way of making loads of new contacts.

There are a variety of speed-dating methods. The one we've used for our events involved about 40 men and women turning up at a bar furnished with tables for two. The Master or Mistress of Ceremonies is in charge of the music which is turned off at intervals for three minutes. In these intervals, couples pair off, according to a prearranged plan, at the tables with their drinks. It's a bit like musical chairs.

With a bit of practice, you soon get into the rhythm of ice-breaking, flirting and finding out a surprising amount about your speed dates in the limited time slots. If you think there's a glint of interest both ways – and you're a fast mover – you can discreetly exchange mobile-phone numbers on the spot (but don't give a terrestrial number, as I have said before, because your address might be traced from it). Some women I've met have had cards printed with just their first name and mobile number – very useful for dating situations. However, what you're really supposed to do if you want to stay in touch is to put a tick against your datee's name on a special card which the organizers scrutinize after the event. If one of your dates has also put a tick against your name then, bingo, you're each sent the other's e-mail address. Speed dating is tremendous fun and, because its purpose is to go for volume, you can practise Domino Dating and spread your net wide.

What's best for you?

The next Workout is to get you thinking about the full spectrum of singles' dating organizations. Through the process of building up a good information base of what is locally available, you can find out what they might have to offer you.

Mansearch Workout – Where to meet your man

Look up dating agencies, dining clubs and events in your local paper, in magazines or on the internet. Which might be the most congenial and appropriate ones for you? Write down the details here. Find out as much as you can about the age group, social background and interests of members and users.

1) ....

2) ....

3) ....

4) ....

5) ....

Personal ads and voicemail dating – opportunities by the pageful

Meeting through personal ads must be one of the best-kept secrets in town. It is amazing how many people read the personal ads. They are not for a minority of loners and losers, as outdated stereotypes would have us believe. On the contrary, you may well know several quite 'normal' people who regularly use personal ads but who haven't told you because they fear your ridicule.

Contrary to popular mythology, people who advertise in these columns are (for the most part) sane, happy and attractive. You may have to steer around the occasional oddball, but the next person you meet through a personal ad could be your future partner. People who do 'personals' usually have lots going on in their lives. They're not sitting around and brooding. They're taking control.

In the old days one would respond to a personal ad using one's best handwriting and paper. Nowadays the most that is usually required is a telephone and a quiet moment to record an intriguing message to be retrieved by the advertiser using their PIN. If they like what they hear, they can leave their own message in reply.

This is great for the super-adventurous, but it is wise to be cautious as there is no personal screening. With some voice-mail dating systems, placing an ad is free and they make their money solely from the premium rate telephone calls made to listen to ads and retrieve messages. Be warned – this can result in enormous phone bills!

Does it work? It is true that a lot can be revealed about a person through accent, intonation and vocabulary, but voices can also be misleading. It is another way of meeting more interesting men. As always, follow my safety recommendations when you decide to contact and advertiser.

SMART BIOG: Angela's telephone tale

A friend of mine, Angela, did a voice-mail advert from her daily broadsheet and was completely won over on the phone by the deep, seductive voice of Keith who answered the ad. They spent hours on the phone 'discovering' one another. After each call Angela would tell me that she had a strong feeling he could be 'the one'. His voice was deep and resonant and made her go weak at the knees. He asked her lots of fascinating questions about herself – a great listener. And they had everything in common – it was meant to be. But for some puzzling reason, Keith didn't suggest meeting up till they had been flirting on the phone for a month. When they finally dated ... well, what can I say? His body had been honed only in the way a lifetime of fast food can achieve. The seductive voice was obviously the result of smoking 40 Gauloise a day, and it in no way compensated for his nicotine-stained fingers and smelly clothes. His physical presence was so much in her face that she kept moving her chair back. In short, Angela couldn't terminate the date quickly enough. Use voice-mail dating by all means, but just don't fall in love with the voice before you've met the person. This sort of situation is unlikely to arise where an agency or friend has vetted men for you.

L♡vebyte

> ❝ No woman should ever be quite accurate about her age – it looks so
> calculating ❞
> Oscar Wilde

The wording of your ad is crucial. You can so easily play into the hands of prejudice. For example, don't put your age in the ad if you're over 40. Just specify the age of the man you are seeking. If you are asked on the phone how old you are, play the bashful female and say that you have a policy of never revealing your age on the phone. Once you meet up and wow him with how wonderful you are, the ageism thing becomes less significant. Age giveaways include saying 'young looking' in your ad – which means you're over 50, or 'young at heart' – which definitely suggests someone over 60.

A phrase used in personal ads that is often misunderstood is 'fun-loving' – some men read it to mean that you prefer to spend all your free time frolicking between the sheets. As you see, it's important to avoid potential double meanings.

L♡vebyte

" Can someone make my simple wish come true?
Male biker seeks female for touring fun.
Do you live in North London? Is it you?
Gay vegetarian whose friends are few,
I'm into music, Shakespeare and the sun.
Can someone make my simple wish come true?
Please write (with photo) to Box 152.
Who knows where it might lead once we've begun?
Can someone make my simple wish come true?
Do you live in North London? Is it you? "
Wendy Cope, from 'Lonely Hearts'

SMART BIOG: Sarah's ad snares architect

Sarah, a 38-year-old paediatrician, found that her long-term partner had left her for another woman. She came to see me, just for a chat, about the possibility of joining up, but we found we didn't have enough suitable men living near her new posting which was well out of town. Her job was very demanding and left her with little energy to spend on herself. She'd always had a poor opinion of people who used personal ads and would never have dreamed of doing it herself.

However, after discussing the idea of personal ads with me, she mentioned it to her flatmate, Jonathon. He was also a good and determined friend and he organized a small ad in a quality weekend newspaper for her as a surprise birthday present. It ran as follows:

'Attractive, slim, blonde, professional woman 38 seeks witty, wise and wonderful man to share country weekends, theatre and eating out. Box no. 280'.

Pretty clichéd? Yes, and it did make her fume! But then, when she received a post-bag of over 30 letters (this was before voice personals), she couldn't help being intrigued – and she read them all. She kept re-reading them and wondering whether she dared phone any of the writers.

There was a letter from a 38-year-old architect who sounded her type – rather extrovert and loved dancing, travel and the country. Although she feared the worst, she finally plucked up the courage to ring him and arranged to meet him at a café in the park one Sunday afternoon. Well, the meeting ended with a promise to get together a week later. Then, they went on a walk in the country, following this with supper in an old country pub with the mandatory log fire.

A year later, Sarah and her architect were living together – and he was the only one she met! Most people, however, have to kiss (or at least meet) a fair number of frogs before they encounter their prince through ads. Labour intensive ads may be, but they do work. In my experience, people who say they don't work are those who take the whole business far too seriously. If they do try them, they usually meet on the first date for too long. A golden rule is that 60–90 minutes is plenty. More than that and awkward silences develop or confessions start to gush out. Keep it short and you will avoid the conversation drifting into such no-go areas such as why your last relationship broke up or how little your therapist understands you!

NB Update: nowadays very few papers and magazines offer the old fashioned, snail mail response to ads – most of them concentrate on voicemail as the response method.

Social Networking Sites

Facebook, MySpace, Bebo – all tremendous fun for organising your social life. My research shows that they are pretty useless for dating. Experts in the field predict that it is more likely that on-line dating agencies will launch their own social networking elements, rather than that social networking sites will start doing dating. But watch this space as change is taking place very rapidly.

What are you waiting for?

There are so many different ways of meeting potential partners! Get strategic, as you would in any other area of your life. Remember that if you don't take any action, nothing in your romance zone is likely to change much. If, on the other hand, you explore new possibilities, even if you don't meet Mr Right, you will at least have moved into dating mode – an important first step in the Domino Dating process.

Keynotes & Diary Prompts

1　Enter in your diary the deadline dates for implementing the next stage of your Mansearch plan and then pick up the phone or the newspaper – or get on the Web – and arrange something now.
2　Safety first. NEVER give a man your address, place of work or terrestrial phone number until you know you can trust him.
3　Get into the spirit of things and just try new options for the hell of it!
4　Tell your friends what you're doing; they'll be impressed and supportive.
5　Complete the Relationship Action Plan below and discuss it with your Dating Buddy.

RELATIONSHIP ACTION PLAN 4

Note down your Smart Action points for the next week:

Positive Action 1:
....
....

Positive Action 2:
....
....

Positive Action 3:
....
....

Treats

Time to treat yourself again – and you can't do it too often. Remember that sex appeal comes down to self-appeal. The more that everything you give to yourself pleases you, the more that everything flowing from you will please everyone else!

♡ *Buy some alluring underwear* and wear it every day – not just on special occasions.

♡ *Test out your perfumes.* Is it time to find something that better expresses this new, confident, great-on-her-own but positively Mansearching woman – or something that brings out another new-flowering aspect of yourself?

♡ Wind down before bedtime by switching off the TV, curling up and *reading that novel,* the one that's been on the shelf for months.

Sarah had always been good at languages – especially translation.

chapter 5

Cyberdating

Spreading your Net worldwide

'Internet dating? Never in a million years!' But wait till you've read this chapter! Dating on the internet is all about availability and usability – anywhere, any time – and so it will widen and multiply your **Domino Dating** opportunities. Cyber-accessibility is phenomenal. You can hook up your laptop wherever there's a telephone or broadband connection or wif-fi. Or just visit your local internet cafe. This means that cyberdating can fit around the lives of busy people and might be something that you should consider – but *alongside* terrestrial opportunities, of course.

Cyberspace encounters – serious or shallow?

In everyday life, as we well know, men and women communicate in different ways. Men have a tendency to share information and facts while women do more of their relating on the emotional level. On-line communication is a wonderful opportunity for men to express themselves emotionally – perhaps for the first time in their lives. They can, through this medium, learn how to connect with others verbally. The power of language, here, is paramount – not the Armani suit or the silver sports car. Acquiring the art of 'courting' in cyberspace is quite a challenge for some men, but they're learning. Old-fashioned love letters are back, albeit in a new guise.

L♡vebyte

❝ When a man gets to talking about himself, he seldom fails to be eloquent and often reaches the sublime. ❞
Josh Billings

In real life, until recently women have had fewer opportunities than men to express their opinions publicly. Now, in cyberspace, they can be bolder and more assertive. Anonymity means that fear of disapproval and censorship is minimized for both sexes. This means that cyber-encounters, although they *can* be trivial, can also be profound and meaningful. They are what you make them.

Electric love – pluses and minuses

The very anonymity of the internet is both its strength and its weakness. Anyone can express themselves without fear, which can be empowering and liberating. On the minus side, there are endless opportunities to present yourself as other than you are. Even this may be a kind of plus as it can give you the possibility of exploring new aspects of your personality which might otherwise have remained dormant. You can practise on the internet. This is what Kate found she was doing ...

SMART BIOG: Kate's cyberdating transformation

Kate, a primary-school teacher, was not one of nature's vamps – quite the contrary: she could never get into flirt mode with men. The fact that they all viewed her as a great chum, but never as potential material for romance, caused her much distress. First dates were rarely followed by second dates. Her body language and style of dressing was prim rather than sexy, *but on the internet no one could see this* and, to her surprise, she found herself caught up in flirtatious e-mailing at an internet dating site without even thinking about it.

For the very first time, Kate felt relaxed in an encounter with a man and it gave her self-esteem an enormous boost. This was the beginning of a new era. Kate started to be more daring in the way she dressed and became less inhibited about real-life flirting. There was another plus for her: currently, there are near enough equal numbers of men and women in internet dating sites, but in terrestrial agencies there can be more women as they like the added security and greater selectiveness. Clever women are cottoning on, however, and the man/woman ratio is changing even as I write. So, if you're a woman who could benefit from a bit of flirt practice, loosen up and let go with some internet encounters.

The fact that you can log on at any time means that you can 'socialize' at the drop of a hat. Sitting in front of your computer screen, in your favourite dressing gown and fluffy puppy-dog slippers, you can feel like a million dollars as you cavort by e-mail with a prospective date on an internet dating site.

'But isn't this evading real life?' It may be – if you become addicted to relating *solely* on the Web. However, it can kick-start your mood. It can get you hungry and ready for real-life encounters – which may well take off from Web connections, too. If you've never explored the possibilities, and don't know where to start, the following sections explain what to go for and what to avoid.

Internet dating agencies – where the cyberaction is at

What an impact internet dating sites have made on the lives of so many people! Who can resist the possibility of being able to 'browse' through profiles of men from the comfort and secrecy of one's own home?

If you're a cyber cynic, think again, or better still, check over your preconceptions by taking a look at what's on offer. If you're really reluctant, you can kid yourself that you're only doing it on behalf of a friend. Yes, some internet sites do attract time-wasters and married men, that's always a risk; and many online agencies will be too lightweight to have the calibre of men you'd like to meet, but there are some gems out there.

L♡vebyte

❝ Before you meet your handsome prince, you have to kiss a lot of toads. ❞
Anon

How do you tell which are the good ones? Look carefully at the kind of questions they expect you to answer on the members' profile; are they likely to elicit an interesting self-portrait – one that will help you find the right sort of guy? For example, some agencies just request details of age, height, job, body shape, hair and skin colour plus one or two details of 'hobbies' and activities. Such a profile might be the sum of the least interesting things about you, rather than a valuable list of your key mate-matching criteria. In **SmartDating.co.uk**, the site I started for readers of this book, we attract educated and lively singles, so, for our staggeringly accurate compatibility questionnaire, we ask all sorts of life-style and value questions to illustrate this. You can see what newspaper the man reads, whether he likes cooking or enjoys scuba diving, and whether his type of humour will make you laugh. The profiles are fascinating to read – very insightful and humorous – and result in intriguing matches. Shop around, before you decide on your internet dating site – and have fun!

Confidentiality is assured as messages are normally sent through the agency's private and secure messaging system – don't be tempted to bypass this. The agency will know your e-mail address, but members won't, as a rule, unless *you* give it out in one of your messages which is strictly against the rules of many sites.

Avoiding cybercreeps

If you go the internet route, you need to stick at it and you must expect to embark on the odd false trail. Keep uppermost in your mind that you're dealing with total strangers and that the internet site in question won't normally have any proof of identity before accepting a member. You must, therefore, be doubly careful about personal safety. NEVER give your terrestrial phone number, your address, place of work or e-mail to a man before you are quite sure you can trust him and you have proof of his identity. Always meet in a public place and have your own transport to and from a date.

At LoveandFriends.com we developed unusual hybrid membership categories to get round the screening and identity problems. Some LoveandFriends Internet Dating members *have*, in fact, also been interviewed and their ID documents recorded at our office. They are identified as 'ID checked' on their profiles. We believe that this original approach will overcome the reticence that some women have about internet dating. It combines the volume element from the internet with the screening process of a selective, personal introduction agency.

Be aware, also, that cyberdating is by no means free of the hazards inherent in other forms of dating. You might think, for instance, that the internet, being at one remove from real life, would have a built-in emotional buffer; but people tell me that cyber-rejection is still painful. The unanswered e-mail can cause as much anguish as the phone that never rings. Forewarned is forearmed.

In spite of these reservations, millions of people worldwide are using internet dating sites as a means of meeting the partner they would never otherwise come across. With minimal initial effort, you can make contact with thousands of potential mates. However, do your research carefully and test drive lots of agencies before you decide which one you'll concentrate on. It is great fun – but keep your sense of perspective! Use the internet as a complement to your real life, not as a replacement for it.

Spin some romance with your cyberdating username

Your username is your pseudonym on the internet. For an on-line dating site you need one which is eye-catching and appealing without being too sexually suggestive or you'll get the wrong kind of response. Here are some I've picked at random: 'Dream Chaser', 'Freckles', 'Saffron', 'Curley', 'Zinfandel', 'Cleopatra', 'TigerGirl', 'BatWoman'. You can, of course, use any everyday name you fancy – as long as it's not your own. Remember, this is anonymous and that's why you can be more adventurous – and maybe unveil a whole new side of yourself.

Mansearch Workout – Choosing a username

Start composing 'oomphy', enticing, alluring usernames in readiness for test-driving internet dating sites

1) ....

2) ....

3) ....

4) ....

5) ....

Flirty headlines that work!

The next job is to get working on your internet dating headline which will, if catchy, nudge those men to e-mail in! Humorous, glamorous or romantic is best. Risqué is fine, but crude or sexually suggestive is plain stupid. Here are some headlines to set you thinking about your own:

♡ 'Green-Eyed Girl Seeks Gorgeous Guy'

♡ 'Sexy Scuba Diver Seeks Someone Scrumptious'

♡ 'Where Is My Scarlet Pimpernel?'

♡ 'Ace Quidditch Player Seeks Wizard for Fun and Magic'

♡ 'Awaiting Imminent Arrival of Mr Right'
♡ 'Bacall seeks Bogart'
♡ 'Fly me to the Moon!'

So, just for fun, open a bottle of wine and go a little mad: write some headlines for yourself in the next Workout – maybe with the help of a friend. If you're stuck, look and see what other members of a prospective site have written.

Mansearch Workout – Finding a flirty headline

Fan the flames of romance! Scribble down some imaginative and seductive headlines to use when you are experimenting with internet dating sites.

1) ....

2) ....

3) ....

4) ....

5) ....

Super-cheap cybercourting

Internet dating really *is* inexpensive. Many internet dating sites are free at the point of entry, but you have to pay a modest amount if you wish to send a message to someone – in other words, if you wish to make full use of the system. A few are free even if you do message other members; however, you must pay to be notified whenever someone answering to your specification joins up, or for other interesting and useful features. Nevertheless, fees for internet sites are staggeringly reasonable; even at the top end of the scale, they will rarely cost you more than the price of a week's sandwiches. Do remember, though, that you usually get no personal attention with internet dating, and personal attention can make all the difference. So do consider complementing internet dating with off-line options as well.

SMART BIOG: **Alicia pairs with cybermatch's colleague**

Alicia was a 50-year-old graphic designer who came to see me at Drawing Down the Moon. Unfortunately, at that moment I didn't have enough compatible older men to whom I could introduce her, so, to her great surprise, I suggested internet dating. Why was this her best option? Well, as I have mentioned, unlike with terrestrial agencies, there tends to be a good ratio of men to women in cyberdating! And they're not all techies!

Alicia was dubious about the idea, but I advised her that by using the type of internet dating site which allows a 'browse before you join' facility, she would be able to see if it had her type of men on board before she committed herself. LoveandFriends.com has the tag 'internet Dating for Thinking People' (a euphemism for 'more educated' members) so I felt it was a good choice for Alicia. It's a good idea to look out for such clues about any particular niche that an internet dating site inhabits. Niche internet dating sites are, by their very nature, smaller in overall membership numbers, but the calibre of members is much higher.

Alicia was still unconvinced. 'I don't want my private details to be given to all and sundry', she protested. I explained that on internet dating sites personal details are confidential, and that Alicia's e-mail address would not be given to any members. It would be used by the site either to let her know when there was a message waiting for her on its confidential e-mail system, or so that the site's newsletter could be sent to her. It would be entirely up to Alicia whether she ever divulged her e-mail address, or any other personal information, directly to another member.

I asked Alicia to keep in touch and let me know how she was getting on. She phoned me some months later to tell me she had just moved in with a wonderful man - not someone she met through the internet site but through a work colleague of one of her internet dates. Yes, she'd thoroughly enjoyed flirting by e-mail and she'd met seven of the men she'd corresponded with. In fact, to her surprise, she'd had a great time. She had suspected that one of lovely guy had lied a smidgen about his age, but the others were all genuine and interesting and two are still good friends - including the one whose colleague she'd fallen in love with! It's that **Domino Dating** business again ...

L♡vebyte

" When a woman really does love a man, he can make her do anything she wants to. **"**

Anon

To post, or not to post, your photo ...

Our research shows that people with photos posted on their profile get seven to ten times the response rate of those who don't. This clearly demonstrates that it's definitely worth posting a photo, providing you've got one that's flattering and gives out the right messages. It would even be worth getting a friend to take one especially for your internet dating adventures.

Remember that photos bleach you out ferociously, so even if you don't wear much make-up, it is worth getting made up for the 'shoot'; it won't be noticed and it will make a huge difference to how you look. Eye make-up will help you emphasize your most important expressive feature, and powder will get rid of the shine that highlights all the wrinkly bits. Don't forget to smile and look at the camera! This could be a 'virtual' first meeting with your future partner, and first impressions can be very persuasive!

Mansearch Workout – Choosing an internet dating site

Check out the major search engines such as Google and Yahoo for details of internet dating sites. You can also look in the dating columns in newspapers and magazines and on the internet. Research what's available and which seem the best for you. Write down the details here. Find out as much as you can about the type of members recruited by each of your entries by inspecting their profiles – if the site allows this before registering.

1) ....

2) ....

3) ....

4) ....

5) ....

Your internet dating profile – choose your best side!

Most internet sites give you the option of writing something personal about yourself and what you're looking for (in addition to age, sex, height, etc). Ignore this at your peril; it will make a big difference to your response rate if it strikes the right note.

Your internet dating profile should be treated just like a first date. Keep it short and flirty. Give out just enough interesting detail to whet the appetite and get them curious while keeping back some of the good bits – you need some surprises left for your e-mails, or of course for the first date itself. Don't write about any negatives, such as 'finding life a bit empty at present'. You don't want to come across as emotionally needy – men find that very scary. Also, it's best not to talk about anything too intimate, such as wanting to have children soon; wait till you get to know one another first. (There is much more on this in Chapter 7, 'Top Tips for Surviving that First Date'.)

If you get stuck while composing your profile, take a look at those of other members and you'll soon find some inspiration. In short, remember your profile is your 'press release' and thus needs to grab attention without being sensational. Why not show your profile to your Dating Buddy and ask how it comes across?

Chat rooms: great for some – time-wasters for others

These are virtual rooms in cyberspace where people congregate – supposedly to discuss certain themes. There can be 20 or more people in a chat room at any one time. Sometimes the conversation takes off, and then it can be interesting, but mostly it just doesn't take off. If you want to get to know a chat-room member a bit better, you can invite them into a 'private room' and chat one-to-one.

My research tells me that chat rooms are great time-wasters and are mostly geared to teenagers. A lot of what passes for 'chat' is rubbish-speak and very childish. A number of providers are withdrawing, or considering withdrawing, their chat facilities because of their abuse by paedophiles. As the availability and calibre of chat rooms is in a constant state of flux you need to do your research very carefully indeed.

To get into a chat room, log on to one of the big providers such as Yahoo and see what headings, if any, they have relating to chat rooms. You'll probably have to provide a user ID and a password. You can then click on a chat room that sounds interesting and just join in – it's all self-explanatory. The 'chat' can either be written or vocal, providing you've downloaded the software to enable using your own voice. Don't worry, it will be offered to you as part of the process.

It can come as a shock to find that some of the visitors who inhabit chat rooms can be gratuitously aggressive or excessively sexually suggestive. It's not uncommon for chat-room users to masquerade under all sorts of aliases and even pretend to be of the opposite sex. Be warned.

Do read all the cautionary words about personal safety outlined below. They are usually also available to you on any chat site when you log in. Put safety first and NEVER give away any personal information. Remember, even if the site is monitored there is no watertight vetting procedure to screen you from someone with evil intent. If you experience anything scary or truly unpleasant in a chat room, then e-*mail the internet Service Provider straightaway.*

If you feel that chat rooms are the thing for you, and you have loads of time to waste, go for them. However, I think you'll meet many more people who are interesting and available through on-line dating sites and your terrestrial opportunities.

Cyberdating safety checks

1 Be especially wary about giving away information that could jeopardize your safety – phone number, address or employer.
2 Ensure you read an internet dating site's terms and conditions of membership before you register.
3 Be sensible about picking a user name – avoid those that are even remotely sexually suggestive or imply vulnerability. You'll be flooded with unappetizing interest if you overlook this tip!
4 Don't give out your personal e-mail address to people you don't know you can trust unless you have checked out what, if any, personal information is linked to your address. For example, if you're away, do you have an out-of-office, automatic e-mail reply containing details about yourself or the company you work for? This may not be the sort of information you want a stranger to have.
5 Although the provider who supplies your e-mail address is supposed to keep confidential any information you have given them about yourself, such as address or phone number, it is theoretically possible (though extremely unlikely) that this can be accessed by unauthorized individuals. Be safe. Think before you divulge personal data.
6 If you have children, be aware that they can be unwittingly drawn into very unpleasant and dangerous liaisons through access to chat rooms and internet dating. Unlike you, they will not necessarily have the judgement or experience to be discriminating. Ensure you take precautions against this by diligently monitoring their computer access.
7 Always read and abide by the safety code on the site.

S⊙undbyte – Cyberflirting

An enormous plus for cyberdating is that you can hone your flirting skills on a daily basis and this is a great confidence builder.

Coming down off the screen – from virtual to actual

Whatever means you use to create dating opportunities, remember that it's important to keep yourself active to maintain the momentum. Ensure you network with lots of people. The internet is just one way of doing this and is excellent if you have very little time or unsociable hours, but don't use it to the exclusion of all else. If you stay at home and brood, you'll be giving out all the wrong messages when you do meet someone and you won't be successful in following the encounter with a further date. On the other hand, if you must spend time at home, use it creatively to ensure that when you do get out you've already set up lots of dating possibilities.

As with terrestrial dating, be a little mysterious at first. Hold on to some choice information about yourself until you talk on the phone or meet; you'll be glad you kept some ice-breakers in reserve. When you finally meet your internet date in the flesh, forget about love at first sight. Instead, ask yourself, is he an interesting person and could he widen your network of friends? Practice Domino Dating, meet every possible man and, just when you're not expecting it, lightning will strike.

Do you want to make that relationship happen? Then get moving on this easy, fun way of adding to your repertoire of dating opportunities. Be cyberactive! Remember, no action – no man.

Keynotes & Diary Prompts

1 If you've never logged on to an internet dating site suspend your prejudices and check out several. Do the last Workout – there's no time like the present!
2 Don't be put off by the fact that there are some loners and weirdos on the Net. There are heaps of interesting, attractive people too.
3 Use internet dating as an adjunct to 'real life' dating, not as a substitute for it.
4 Make a prominent 'Safety first' entry in your Workbook:

'Until I *know for sure* that I can trust a man, I will:

♡ ONLY send mesages through the confidential e-mail service of the internet dating site and not my own e-mail;

♡ ALWAYS meet him in a public place;

♡ ALWAYS have (and use) my own transport home;

♡ NEVER give him my address, my place of employment or terrestrial phone number.'

5 You can find matches for your single friends at internet dating sites. Then e-mail the usernames of these 'finds' to them, so that they can take a look.

6 Remember that those who take the dating process too seriously are doomed to failure. Have fun – and don't try too hard!

RELATIONSHIP ACTION PLAN 5

Note down your Smart Action points for the next week:

Positive Action 1:

....

....

Positive Action 2:

....

....

Positive Action 3:

....

....

Treats

♡ Supposing it's Tuesday tomorrow, *plan a treat-for-two* (you and a friend or a date) for tomorrow – and for the following three Tuesdays. It doesn't have to be the same friend – or the same treat – but it might be nice ...

♡ On the way to work, *buy a pretty plant for your desk or office windowsill.* To have something alive and natural near us, particularly in cities, is both a TREAT and a necessity. Besides which, research has shown that placing a plant where you can see it increases your productivity by 12%.

♡ *Arrange to meet a friend at your favourite restaurant.* TREAT yourself to sharing with them all your favourite dishes.

Friends were surprised by Caroline's sudden interest in scuba diving and hi-fis.

chapter 6

Preparing to Date Successfully

The essential challenge for Mansearchers

Hundreds of books have been written on 'How to Get Your Man Now!', 'How to Build up Your Confidence', 'How to Feel Really Attractive' and 'How to Feel Flirty'. How many such books have you seen? Indeed, how many have you bought? Why, though, do they so often fail to produce results? I'll tell you why. They concentrate so much on buffing up your confidence that they overlook the all-important fact that there may still be some other things about you that are turning prospective suitors away – negative things you would change *if* you were aware of them. This chapter rises to that challenge. It will help you to zap, or at least minimize, anything which might be a potential turn off.

What your best friend won't tell you

Skip this chapter – and the next – if you don't think that a date could change the rest of your life. Skip them if the *right* men always find you attractive and interesting.

On the other hand, stay with these chapters if you think you could benefit from some insights about dating turn-ons and turn-offs. Perhaps you think you know what yours are? Take my advice – think again! Many of us have no real idea of what others find attractive or unattractive about us. We don't know how others actually see us – mainly because we don't ask them, or else we don't ask them in the right way. Even when we do sense that we're giving out the wrong signals, we still don't know how to change them.

I'm not talking here about fundamentals, but about small things that you could easily begin to tackle – if you were sufficiently aware and determined.

To get some sense of this, see how many of the following statements you can answer with conviction:

Mansearch Workout – How I appear to dates ...

	Yes	No
I come across as emotionally balanced (not emotionally needy).	☐	☐
They find my conversation intriguing and interesting (not monotonous or frivolous).	☐	☐
They like the way I make eye contact (not too intrusive nor too detached).	☐	☐
When I ask questions, I always wait for an answer.	☐	☐
They find my jokes are highly entertaining.	☐	☐
They always feel I am talking with them (not at *them*).	☐	☐
My laughter is infectious (not irritating).	☐	☐
I never suffer from bad breath.	☐	☐
My body language shows me to be fit, youthful and confident (not worn-out and defeated).	☐	☐
I wear clothes that express my personality and I look good to others.	☐	☐

Surprised? Unsure? Of course there are big issues lurking in these seemingly simple questions, but also lots of small but significant issues for would-be daters. Now is the time to become more aware of how people read you by seeking feedback whenever possible. You can then decide what, if anything, needs reviewing.

Use your imagination when doing the Workouts that follow, and see if you can get your Dating Buddy to join in. The idea is to establish exactly what messages others are picking up from you through your body language and general presentation. You can bet your bottom dollar that whatever you are like in everyday life you'll be more so on that first date – and it will matter. It may be, for instance, that you talk too much, have a limp handshake, gappy teeth or an unflattering hairstyle. All these relatively minor blemishes can be rectified – and they need to be, if you want to get to a second date.

L♡vebyte

" From looking, men get to loving. **"**
Clement of Alexandria

SMART BIOG: **Avoiding Angela**

Angela, an attractive secondary-school teacher whom I knew before I started matchmaking professionally, met lots of men through personal ads. She would phone to give me the low-down on her latest date, often reporting that it had gone really well and that she had high hopes of their meeting up again. But did they? No. The next time we spoke I would hear that the man in question hadn't called or that, when she'd called him, he'd said he was 'rather tied up with work at the moment'. She had the opportunities, she was ready for a relationship, she was attracted to the men she met and she was attractive herself, but nothing ever developed. It wasn't a question of not meeting any men, and it wasn't that they were the wrong type. The problem was that *they were turned off*.

Angela read lots of relationship books, but to no avail. What was she doing that blew her chances? We, her friends, all guessed – but did any of us say anything? No, friends rarely do! The problem was this: since her divorce, and living on her own, Angela had got into the habit of talking non-stop when she was with anyone so that it was impossible to get a word in edgeways. She was effusive, intense and exhausting to be with. The keener she was on a man, the worse she'd be – through nervousness and wanting to be liked. It was no surprise that they didn't want to see her again. She was giving out messages that overwhelmed whoever she was with – and she didn't realize it. Today, many years on, she is still looking for someone special. No one, including me, felt it was their business to tell Angela.

Getting help with the tough stuff

Maybe Angela's problem with men was something she could have successfully overcome on her own had she become aware of it. If one of her friends had said 'Hold on a moment, Angela, if you come over less effusively, perhaps do a bit more listening' then she would have taken it on board. Mostly, however, we put up with the faults of our friends and feel that it would be interfering to discuss them: but, if you ask your friends and work colleagues in the right way, they *will* give you the feedback you need to drop any irritating or unattractive habits.

Maybe, on the other hand, Angela's problems were so deep that they needed some professional help. And so a word of advice here: I do urge you to consider psychotherapy or counselling if you feel you may be sabotaging your chances out of profound insecurity, fear of rejection, terror of being hurt – or any other overwhelming emotion. A difficult childhood, or problematic relationship with a parent or other loved one, can create wounds severe enough to need outside help to heal them.

L♡vebyte

66 It's better to be looked over than overlooked. 99
   Mae West

Top turn-off triggers

These talking therapies are, however, unlikely to help you much with the more subtle dynamics of dates. A therapist won't usually see their client socializing – this would not be part of the job, so you need to find out for yourself. You may, for instance, be discouraging people from wanting to explore a relationship with you by using negative, 'go-away' body language that you learned in your teens when it was cool. You may be using other turn-off habits such as talking too much about yourself, invading the other person's personal space, being a bad listener or, like Angela, just being too intense. For all of us, habitual patterns of sabotaging behaviour may linger long after the psychological causes have been dealt with – and we may be completely unaware of this.

Put deep issues on the back burner and look at how people react when they first meet you. We all know that first impressions can label someone instantly as a romance or friendship candidate who's worth further consideration.

Such factors as time-warped clothes, hairstyle or make-up can mask attractiveness in an otherwise attractive person. Body language and voice may also be sending out the wrong signals. 'But wait a minute', you may be thinking, 'if a man can't see past these trivial things and appreciate me for what I really am, then he's not for me'. Wrong – absolutely wrong. In my experience, interesting and sensitive guys are just as likely to be discouraged by superficial details as the unattractive ones. I find there are no exceptions to this; and top turn-offs on first dates are mostly things that you would and could change if you knew about them.

L♡vebyte

66 'I'm tired of all this nonsense about beauty being only skin deep ...'
'What do you want – an adorable pancreas?' 99
Jean Kerr

Faulty self-image?

You'd be surprised and shocked to know that friends often see you completely differently to the way you see yourself. However, unless you have a very open and special relationship with them, they would never dream of saying so. The result: faulty self-image or FSI as we call it at Drawing Down the Moon.

An interesting example of faulty self-image is that virtually every person who comes through our doors confides to us that they 'know' they look at least five years younger than they are. The reason? Their friends say this to them on birthdays or when looking at photos to make them feel good (which in turn makes the friends feel good). Even your frankest, closest friend isn't going to burst this little bubble for you! Your very best friends are the ones most likely to collude with your FSI. Do *you* really believe you look younger than you are? Honest now – own up! I do, and *I* know all about FSI!

L♡vebyte

66 A woman is as old as she looks to a man who likes to look at her. 99
Finley Peter Dunne

A paradoxical feature of faulty self-image is that we can be convinced by our rose-tinted vision of ourselves while, at the same time, suffering low self-esteem. At the agency, we occasionally get some averagely attractive applicants who *say* they lack confidence in themselves. And yet (and this never fails to surprise us) these people still routinely believe that the potential dates whom *they* fancy – people who are much more attractive than *they* are – will want to meet *them*. It's a tricky one for us to deal with without hurting their feelings. If someone fancies a potential partner who is way ahead of them in the attraction stakes, then it's unlikely we can help.

The Date Doctor

A novel way of getting feedback about how others see you is the **Date Doctor** project we've been experimenting with. Now and again we find that someone is in need of a bit of extra feedback of the sort they're unable to get from everyday sources. They may be unable to fathom why people they meet tend to misread them. To this small, quite brave group of people we may suggest a session with the Date Doctor. This can be the beginning of an exciting voyage of personal discovery.

Here's how it works. Our **curious dater** meets with the Date Doctor – an experienced cognitive psychotherapist – to discuss what he or she hopes to achieve. When the dater feels ready, a light-hearted 'date' is arranged with the datee – usually a trainee psychotherapist of the opposite sex and similar age. The idea is to create, as far as possible, the ambience of a social, rather than a clinical, meeting. Obviously, it's not the same as real life, but people who've participated in the arrangement have reported that it all seems surprisingly natural and relaxed: 'Like a chat with a good friend', reported one member. If it turns out to be a bit stressful – then all well and good; first dates *are* a bit stressful.

After the 'date', the datee writes up a report that is then discussed with the curious dater at a further session with the psychotherapist. The brief for the Date Doctor is: first, to build confidence around the positive aspects of your interaction with others and, only then, to address problem areas in whatever ways are most appropriate. From this you can gain incredibly useful insights into your social self.

SMART BIOGs: Mary-Ann, Linda and Denzil successfully update

One Date Doctor client, Mary-Ann, a successful barrister who found that first dates rarely translated into second dates, said she had no idea that she was avoiding direct eye contact with her datee – probably a hangover from the time she was a shy, only child. She was also astounded to learn that he found her wardrobe old fashioned and un-sexy. Eye-avoidance and 'granny' clothes are both sizeable turn-offs.

Denzil, a writer of television dramas had also consulted the Date Doctor because his dates never seemed to go anywhere. He reported that he was unaware that he interrupted his datee so often. He was pleased that she found him entertaining nevertheless.

Linda, an academic also with no follow-through on dates, was delighted to learn that she came across as a thoroughly interesting and amusing person who seemed concerned and curious about her datee's opinions and feelings. However, one minor but important bit of feedback was that she had an extremely irritating nervous sniff that needed dealing with – and about which she was completely unaware! Can you imagine Marilyn Monroe or Michelle Pfeifer with a sniff?

In real life, who is going to tell these people about these little and not-so-little turn-offs? Mary-Ann, Linda and Denzil all immediately jumped on their off-putting habits and presentation and said they only wished someone had told them before. But if they had been able to ask their friends about how they came across, they would probably have nipped their off-putting habits in the bud.

What about starting, right now, on the enriching process of becoming your own Date Doctor? To do this, you are going to need to be business-like about how you obtain and organize the material with which you need to work. It is also very important that you have a structure on which you can peg all the different aspects of your Date Doctor strategy. To help you, I have borrowed from the world of commerce a useful tool known as **SWOT analysis**.

SWOT your way to romance

Marketing consultants who are trying to analyse the prospects of a new product or service, conduct a SWOT analysis. **SWOT** stands for:

Strengths;

Weaknesses;

Opportunities;

Threats.

All of these are examined in depth before determining a marketing strategy for the new venture.

I asked Alison, a marketing consultant, to give me an illustrative example of SWOT analysis. She chose Coca-Cola and explained that a SWOT analysis would suggest that by far the greatest of its Strengths is its strong brand identity – in other words, Coke is known to be satisfying, enjoyable and to taste the same wherever you are. Its biggest Weakness is its high sugar content and thus its potential for rotting teeth. Its Opportunities might involve maintaining high esteem and brand loyalty through sponsorship, youth-support schemes and competitions. Finally, Coca-Cola's Threats may include other high-energy brands taking over the market.' That is SWOT analysis applied commercially. The Mate Market demands no less rigour.

Now, I am not advocating anything so crass as viewing yourself simply as a brand to be marketed. The problem, however, with some of the wonderfully successful women (and men) who come to see me is that they have hitherto been reluctant to apply to their personal lives the same useful, common-sense tools and strategies that have helped them achieve so much at work.

'Get strategic', now, and employ this SWOT approach in evaluating the changes you need to make to achieve a goal more important to you than any work project or deadline – an enduring personal relationship. What are your Strengths, Weaknesses, Opportunities and Threats?

Do the following SWOT Workouts with the help of a friend and you'll get further faster. Some courageous women I know have done this sort of exploration with an ex-partner. This, however, is appropriate only if you are good friends and have sorted out all the unfinished business.

Brief your helper carefully. You want them to be 100% honest and not collude with your Weaknesses. But also ask them to give you, say, three positive chunks of feedback for every negative chunk. This understanding is really important. If you haven't got a friend to help, just imagine you are in your date's shoes, and he is writing about you – and be honest! Start with your Strengths, to put you in a positive frame of mind.

SWOT 1 – your Strengths scrutinized

What are the things that are great about you? What are those positive aspects of you and your personality that you'd like your potential partner to appreciate and eventually love? If you are doing this exercise on your own, make a list of all the things that have ever attracted you to someone else – energy, curiosity, enthusiasm, sense of fun, intelligence, etc. Next, see which ones you reckon are your own strong points. This is not a time for modesty. Try and step outside yourself for a moment. If you get stuck, imagine you are being described by your best friend.

Mansearch Workout – My Strengths

Some lucky man is getting a woman who is:

1) ....

2) ....

3) ....

4) ....

5) ....

People have many kinds of wonderful qualities – and there are just as many with which we don't resonate at all. Here is a list that may help you to remember a goodly number of yours.

Positive-Quality Suggestions

Energetic	Supportive	Gets things done
Generous	Witty	Good-natured
Kind	Physical	Genuine
Deeply committed	Happy	Tender
Extroverted	Liberal	Loving
Adventurous	Modest	Self-respecting
Tolerant	Sensual	Relaxed
Dedicated	Sharing	Strong
Good flirt	Honest	Caring
Creative	Sophisticated	Intelligent

Great cook	Fun	Insightful
Affectionate	Efficient	Beautiful
Warm	Smart	Imaginative
Cheerful	Laid-back	Gregarious
Communicative	Light-hearted	Talented
Compassionate	Stylish	Confident
Sympathetic	Interested	Gentle
Optimistic	Nurturing	Practical
Thoughtful	Idealistic	Playful
Bright	Joyful	Lovely voice
Sexy	Discerning	Pretty
Appreciative	Contemplative	Deep-thinking
Intuitive	Sociable	

SWOT 2 – Get wise to your Weaknesses

You've now given yourself a few well-deserved strokes. Hang on to these while we confront the negatives: those Weaknesses that can be date-destroyers. Choose a moment when you feel *really* good about yourself to do the next exercise.

Mansearch Workout – My Weaknesses

Date One may not become Date Two because:

1) ....

2) ....

3) ....

4) ....

5) ....

Again, if you haven't got someone to work with you on this, think of the people who have put *you* off and ask yourself: 'Am I ever like that?' These off-putting people may be moaners, put-down artists, prickly, opinionated, hyper-critical or they might prattle on about their work. Sometimes it really is in someone's nature to be like this; others may be OK for most of the time and it's simply the stress of a new encounter (with all its hidden agendas) that causes them to revert to old patterns of behaviour. First dates show up the Achilles' heel in all of us – after all, it's a bit like being tested in an exam. Do you behave differently on first dates? How does any nervousness express itself?

Off-Putting Characteristics?

The following list may help to remind you of some of your more spectacular Weaknesses:

Impatient	Needs to impress	Intense
Arrogant	A moaner	Negative body language
Doesn't pamper self	Can't relax	Hypercritical
A slave to routines	Dogmatic	Avoids commitments
Too intense	Over-emotional	Irresponsible
Obsessed with success	Always needs approval	No sense of style
Generally obsessive	Self-obsessed	Puts themselves down
Manipulative	Needs to be needed	No 'get up and go'
Domineering	Badly groomed	Talks with mouth full
Overweight	Jealous	Lacks spontaneity
Likes to feel martyred	Bad breath	A guilt-tripper
Over-perfectionist	Undermining	Unflattering hair style
A put-down artist	Flirts too much	Sexually inhibited
Neurotic	Opinionated	Unable to share
Selfish	Lacks originality	Can't keep secrets
Bad eye contact	Conceited	Body odour
Emotionally inhibited	Always right	Bad posture
Doesn't listen	Takes offence easily	Unable to flirt
Inconsiderate	Sarcastic	Indecisive
Disorganized	Possessive	Bites nails
Tries too hard	Inappropriate dress	Ungenerous
Doesn't ask questions	Discontented	Unsympathetic
Voice-work needed	Feels rejected	

The next job is to sort these Weaknesses into different categories, because you will be thinking about working on them in different ways. File them under one of the following three headings:

1 Bad habits;
2 Off-putting visual messages;
3 Deep emotional programming.

1 Bad habits

Herein lie all the tendencies and 'action patterns' which are behavioural reflections of your early emotional programming. Underlying insecurities and anxieties may result in a tendency to sound defensive or to control situations. Desperately wanting to be liked might be causing you to talk a great deal or to compromise your own wants and needs in order to please your date or partner.

Negative body language, such as stooping or always folding your arms – which probably you are quite unaware of – sends out strong 'she's-got-problems' signals to those around you. These habits may continue even after any deeper problems have been confronted and more or less resolved. An excessive desire to be liked, for example, which may have arisen through early insecurity, can manifest as smiling too readily, even though you now feel confident and appreciated most of the time. The man you're dating might well want to run a mile if he reads this as a sign of emotional neediness.

I discovered that I was a 'smiler' when I went on a management course as part of my old job in adult education. We all watched videos of ourselves role-playing various scenarios, from trying to resolve a conflict situation between two members of staff to negotiating with the union. I was horrified at how often and how inappropriately I smiled. I discussed it with my group and we agreed that I gave off too many 'wanting to be liked' messages which undermined my authority. Not even my best friends had ever mentioned this tendency to me, but they had noticed it and thought about it privately – which I discovered on talking to them after the course.

I still smile rather readily, but I now know that it's not the best way of dealing with stressful situations. Of course, it's good to smile when you *really* want to, and at the agencies we have a lot of evidence which shows that people who look happy in their photographs get picked more often; so keep a good balance between the two extremes.

L♡vebyte

❝ It is only shallow people who do not judge by appearances. **❞**
Oscar Wilde

2 Off-putting visual messages

This section houses such counterproductive items as an unflattering hairstyle or a time-warped wardrobe – which are relatively easy to rectify.

SMART BIOG: Jeanette's story

Five years ago a friend of mine, Jeanette, asked her long-term partner to move out of the house they shared when she discovered he was having an affair with another woman. In an effort to kick his memory out of her mind, she threw out lots of the things they had bought together and she then redecorated the house. She also cut her hair really short, and I mean *short*. Her ex-partner had loved her wavy, shoulder-length hair, and getting it cut was, in a way, to spite him. Her friends (mostly women) said the new style really suited her, as friends invariably do when you've tried something new with your appearance. As she found it was much easier to maintain, she kept it that way. Recently she told me she'd 'had it' with men, but perhaps they'd 'had it' with her.

Many men – even the progressive, sensitive, 'thinking' types – 'read' cropped hair as a denial of femininity and will say to me, when I show them pictures of fashionable, cropped heads, that they don't feel attracted to 'women like that'. The fact that their short hair (however attractively gamine) consciously or sub-consciously triggers this reaction usually comes as a surprise to those women.

People frequently fail to express their personality in their looks. Their clothes, for instance, may actually deny who they are. Often, they wear garments that are a hangover from an earlier decade of their life. At the agency, if we feel something like this is going to impede their dating progress, we sometimes refer them (if we feel they are open to the suggestion) to our image consult-ant. This is *not* to graft on a new look, but to advise them how to project them-selves more effectively.

S⊕undbyte – Glasses full time?

A tricky one this but, on first dates, glasses can be a communication barrier. We suggest flirtatiously removing them now and again. Once a man knows you, he seems to get used to the idea of glasses.

Here are a few things which, from our experience, we KNOW lots of men dislike:

- ♡ Highlighted hair – they can think you're going grey!
- ♡ Hair roots needing retouching;
- ♡ Very short hair;
- ♡ Too much make-up;
- ♡ Dangly earrings;
- ♡ Lots of brassy or gold jewellery;
- ♡ Pearls – many men think they look 'Mumsy';
- ♡ Scarves;
- ♡ Baggy clothes;
- ♡ Bad posture;
- ♡ Glasses – a communication barrier at first; flirtatiously whip them off now and again;
- ♡ Overdressing.

L♡vebyte

❝ The high-heeled shoe is a marvellously contradictory item; it brings a woman to a man's height, but makes sure she cannot keep up with him. ❞
Germaine Greer

3 Deep emotional programming

This involves the heavier psychological issues to do with the reasons why you may feel insecure, defensive or unhappy with yourself – which, of course, most of us do at times. If, however, you feel like this constantly, and you believe it is undermining you, then seek professional help.

SWOT 3 – ALL your Opportunities

This exciting and important section of your SWOT analysis will include finding every Opportunity for 'polishing the positives', for making the best of all the really good characteristics you know you possess. To do this effectively, you need to get constructive feedback about yourself whenever possible. Use everyday situations at work or with friends. Ask:

♡ 'Would you like me to change the way I do this?'

♡ 'How do you feel when I say ...?'

♡ 'Give me your opinion of my strategy.'

♡ 'I want your honest verdict on my performance this month.'

♡ 'What do you really think of this dress (hair colour, lipstick ...)?'

If you feel people might not be honest for fear of hurting your feelings, you can avoid putting them in an awkward position by giving them a positive way of handing you the criticism, for instance:

'How would you like me to _improve_ the way I do ...?'

rather than

'What's _wrong_ with the way I do ...?'

This is a much more satisfying question to answer, as everyone loves being helpful. It's also much easier to take on board. Here are several more examples so you can get the drift:

'Should I encourage our friends to talk more when we see them?'

rather than

'Do I talk too much about myself when I'm with them?'

'Do you think a darker shade would suit me better?'

rather than

'Is this shade too light on me?'

'Would you like me to drive more slowly?'

rather than

'Do I drive too fast for you?'

'Do you think I should grow my hair a bit?'

rather than

'Does this hairstyle really suit me?'

'Would you like more time?'

rather than

'Am I pressuring you?'

Become a people watcher and study body language to pick up clues. There are some useful examples in Chapter 7 (hands clasped behind the head, hair patting, fingers at/in mouth, etc – *see* pages 138–39), for surviving that first date, and in Chapter 8 (the flash of a smile, the flicker of a glance, and the lingering gaze – *see* page 165), for serious seduction, to help you get into observer mode.

These are invaluable ways of discovering the things that interest and attract people, as well as the things that turn them off. It should soon become second nature to take stock of how you're coming across in everyday situations so that, when you go on a date, you will know you are giving out the right messages.

L♡vebyte

" A dress has no purpose unless it makes a man want to take it off. **"**
Françoise Sagan

Optimizing your Opportunities

Date school

There is an abundance of Opportunities to participate in courses, groups and workshops that enable us to get a much clearer vision of ourselves – and to take conscious and constructive action as a result. Many of these provide the opportunity for us to recognize our multifarious talents and get them 'moving'. At the same time, they help us recognize our acquired and accumulated self-beliefs that have been holding us back – and get those zapped! Such courses are to be found everywhere, and some of the best are run by local authorities as part of their adult and further-education schemes. However, do also look at what's on offer through your company, professional association or union. Don't be put off if these courses or activities are work-related. The techniques deployed in everyday on-the-job situations can be surprisingly similar to those you might use on a date. This self-observation and self-analysis is valuable in all aspects of our lives and can be especially beneficial in ensuring that first dates *do* turn into second – and third dates.

SMART BIOG: Tooth-shy Susan

Susan, a civil servant, always used to hold her hand in front of her mouth when she talked, which made her difficult to hear and inhibited the communication flow. It was only while on a management-training course, she watched a video of the proceedings that realized this gesture was a problem – and has since stopped doing it. She'd adopted the habit when she was an embarrassed teenager wearing braces to straighten her teeth.

Group insight

Attending personal development courses or workshops provides various bonuses that we can't always get from working by ourselves at home. We may learn how to control anger outbursts, how to give ourselves essential 'time out' through meditation or relaxation exercises, or how to express ourselves more effectively to friends, partners or employers. A course provides the discipline of regular attendance – plus additional 'homework'. The energy generated by the group can also keep you focused and self-aware. You can get valuable feedback from the others. There is also the valuable process which is 'group work' itself.

Group work may, for instance, take the form of role-playing, where challenging issues (sometimes from well back in childhood) can be explored by acting them out with the help of other group members in a supportive environment. This role-play work – or psychodrama, as it is often called – is a method highly valued by class leaders and course tutors of all kinds for providing 'instant insight' into various aspects of our beliefs and behaviour. As a result, these issues often clear by themselves – and then we can move on.

Building assertiveness skills

Assertiveness techniques can be used for both personal and professional effectiveness. The term 'Assertiveness Training' entered the 21st century under something of a cloud because 'assertiveness' was often confused with 'aggressiveness'. The main goal of Assertiveness Training is to be able to express feelings and views directly, clearly and honestly with confidence and assurance. It is definitely *not* about being punitive or bossy, rather it is about being sensitive to yourself as well as about other people and their rights; treating others as equals without putting them down, manipulating them or apologizing for your own behaviour. In Assertiveness Training, three types of behaviour are identified as being typical of those used in situations we deal with badly. These are described as Aggressive, Passive or Manipulative. Often we swing between these alternatives, for example between Passive and Aggressive. Instead of these options, we are encouraged to behave Assertively – with directness and respect for our own feelings and needs as well as those of the other person. If you think that learning more about Assertiveness might be helpful to you, read *A Woman in Your Own Right*, Anne Dickson's great book on the subject, or see if there is a course you can join. This could be a key to getting a promising relationship moving towards a happy ending.

L♡vebyte

" *Dear Zsa-Zsa:* My husband is a travelling salesman, but I know he strays even when he is at home. How can I stop him?
Zsa-Zsa Gabor: Shoot him in the legs. **"**
(Letter to Zsa-Zsa Gabor's top-rating TV show, 'Bachelor's Haven')

Life coaching – a friend for your date with life

A novel approach to self-improvement is Life Coaching. At the agencies, we sometimes refer people to it because it's a great way of getting focused and motivated. Life coaching is something you might like to consider, especially if you need to re-focus your dating skills. A life coach can help you be more fulfilled, balanced and effective. Not only will you be able to achieve transformations in a variety of personal and professional ways, but you will also feel better emotionally.

I have had my own personal life coach and found that my weekly telephone sessions with her were wonderfully energizing. She helped me to find solutions and make the most of my opportunities. She offered alternatives, kept me fixed on my goals and shared her knowledge and experience with me. Think about it as an option that could provide a much-needed catalyst. With the help of a good book on the subject, you could do the job yourself, or else you could splash out on a personal life coach – maybe just for a three-month trial. Some life coaches offer a free telephone taster consultation. It's worth investigating.

Of course, you don't want to become a personal-development junkie. Most of us, though, can benefit from looking inward and acquiring some new personal and presentation skills, so think in terms of 'harvesting' any useful bits from whatever's on offer. There is no area of your life more likely to feel the benefit of this kind of work than the romance zone. Check it out, see what your friends are up to, and list any ideas you could be tempted to explore in this next Workout:

Mansearch Workout – Optimizing your Opportunities

What would help you to optimize your Opportunities?

1) ....

2) ....

3) ....

4) ....

5) ....

Other self-help ideas

To get you in the mood for this assignment, here is a selection of practical suggestions – for mind and body:

- ♡ Public-speaking groups – greater confidence;
- ♡ T'ai chi, yoga and Pilates – be centred, fit and have wonderful posture;
- ♡ Life coaching;
- ♡ Counselling, psychotherapy;
- ♡ Self development classes and books;
- ♡ Exercises, the gym and personal training;
- ♡ Session with a nutritionist;
- ♡ Voice coaching;
- ♡ Slimming club;
- ♡ Image consultation;
- ♡ Free cosmetic-counter makeover;
- ♡ Girlfriend to help turn out wardrobe or go shopping with you;

♡ Visit to local bookshop and stock up on useful books;

♡ Read a good newspaper every day (and always before a date) and keep up with the news and opinion.

Not only will these inject you with more confidence and oomph, but some of them will also provide great opportunities for meeting interesting men. Toastmasters' public-speaking groups, for example, are often used by people needing to hone their presentational skills for careers in business, law, TV, advertising or academia. Toastmasters are to be found all over the world and are always friendly and encouraging. (To explore the possibility of joining your local group, *see* www.toastmasters.org.)

Domino Dynamics

The Domino Dating effect is, I believe, one of the key opportunities for dating success. To remind you once again, with Domino Dating the more dates you have with men who are roughly right, but may not be Mr Perfect, the more confident and positive you'll feel. Also, your network of contacts will grow and you might even end up with your date's brother!

Using the various strategies suggested here for creating Opportunities will help you enormously with the whole business of cultivating a happy-go-lucky approach to dates. These Opportunities will also provide you with many more chances to practise polishing the positives and zapping the negatives. The most important result will be to overcome (or greatly minimize) the biggest obstacle – fear of failure. If you fail with one particular date, you know that there will still be plenty more in the pipeline! Just keep saying 'Next!' if they don't happen to work out.

SWOT 4 – Thrashing the Threats to romance

The biggest general Threats to a successful search for a partner are simple and obvious. Near the top of the list is **leaving everything to fate** and hoping that your romantic life will sort itself out without assistance. Also high on the list is **not getting enough dating practice** – the more dates you have, the more opportunities you'll get to handle your encounters well. Again, it's that Domino Dating effect – so don't be too picky too soon.

Friends who collude with failure are a sure Threat to your relationship opportunities – those moan-and-whinge merchants who drag you down to their level and won't be comfortable seeing you happy. Does this mean dumping some of your best friends? No, just recognize how they're holding you back and regard them as a challenge. Balance out the moaners with encouraging and supportive people. Seek out the company of energizing individuals whom you can regard as role models. Try to discover what *they* did to achieve their goals – after all, this is far better than feeling envious and avoiding them. You'll find they will help to catalyse exciting changes for you.

The biggest single Threat of all to romance is maybe your **career**. For so many women it takes up a disproportionate amount of time and energy, and yet it is the rock upon which the rest of their life is built. Learn to juggle, so that your working life doesn't take over completely. Good luck with this one – it's not easy!

Last but not least is the Threat of **taking things too earnestly**. Cultivate a humorous attitude and don't forget those TREATS!

For this next Workout, consider the various Threats to your love life and ask yourself which you can eliminate.

Mansearch Workout – Threats to my chances for romance

	Yes	No	Will change
Leaving it to fate and doing nothing	☐	☐	☐
Not enough practice at dating	☐	☐	☐
Friends	☐	☐	☐
Career	☐	☐	☐
Taking everything too earnestly!	☐	☐	☐
Other Threats:	☐	☐	☐

....

....

Note: Tackle these Threats with vigour, but, as with all the suggestions in this book, ensure that that you always return to the positives – your Strengths.

To round off this Chapter, look again at your list of Strengths and put it somewhere accessible where you can review it regularly. This list is a personal affirmation – by you, about you. Think of it when you get distracted from your relationship goals. If you are discouraged, remember that positive thinking is neither about ignoring your darker side nor about straining determinedly to eliminate your Weaknesses; it is, rather, about learning to balance the negatives with strong positives. View the items on your Weaknesses list as challenges rather than shackles – and put your main focus on what you want to get out of life.

Visualizing your future

Having become more aware of what you need to do to be more attractive, your next task is to cultivate the belief that you can't fail to find a happy relationship. You need to get into successful dating mode. You need to be able to daydream the successful outcome to your search and do it often. Every time a thought of failure sneaks into your mind, consciously replace it with a vision of success, a happy ending. Get into the habit of doing this and imagine how you look when you are happy in a loving relationship; how you feel – and even conjure up the sound of – your lover's voice and what he is saying. It has to happen in your mind before it can happen in reality.

Think about the goals you need to reach to find a partner. Visualize how your life will change when you achieve them. Think of what you will be doing on a day-to-day basis, of how you will feel and how everything around you will appear. Imagine it as a film in which you are playing the starring role. This technique is advocated by practitioners of Neuro-Lingustic Programming (NLP) and it is a powerful tool for creating the life you want in the way you want it. It can motivate you to create wonderful dating opportunities. It can help you float into 'dating mode'.

However, there's a bit of paradox here. OK, you've stepped into your happy ending film, you've been proactive about your Mansearch strategies and have some great dates to look forward to. In fact, you've got one lined up for tonight. Hold on a minute! Take a deep breath and just let go. Forget the goals and nudge all those Mansearch expectations aside while you are actually *on* the date. You're no longer a woman with a mission. Just enjoy being your attractive self and discover another human being. Ask yourself whether you'd like to see him again and be friends, not whether he measures up to your vision of the future partner. Happy endings in the dating business require careful pacing. Don't say you weren't warned!

Keynotes & Diary Prompts

1 Be brave and be aware – seek out constructive feedback from friends and colleagues on how you come across whenever possible.
2 Explore whether some personal-development techniques could enhance the way you communicate and present yourself.
3 Use everyday encounters to get as much practice as you can in connecting with people, whether or not on a date. The more practice you get, the more likely you'll be to experience the Domino Dating Effect and the less chance you'll have of sabotaging the big dating opportunity.
4 Don't wait for things to happen – because nothing will unless you make it. Big waves of activity start from little ripples, so start stirring!

RELATIONSHIP ACTION PLAN 6

Note down your Smart Action points for the next week:

Positive Action 1:

....

....

Positive Action 2:

....

....

Positive Action 3:

....

....

Treats

♡ It's time for *another massage* (if you didn't book a series during Chapter 2). Or why not trade one with a friend? They might like it if you cooked them dinner or made them a cake.

♡ Go salsa dancing with a friend. Never tried it? Lots of clubs will give lessons for beginners at the beginning of the evening – and who knows what interesting encounters may result.

♡ If it's a good TV night, treat yourself to a *long, lazy home pedicure*.

Tom and Katrina both began to regret exaggerating a love of art in their agency profiles.

chapter 7

Top Tips for Surviving that First Date

Stay calm – it's only a date!

The really proactive woman will look for a positive spin in any situation – and this especially applies to first dates. Please don't try to decide whether you actually fancy him straightaway. Even if he is god's gift to women, there is little chance that on a first date he'll be relaxed enough to dazzle you with all his charisma. Remember, that the same applies to you too, because however easygoing you are, a first date *is* a test. You're both assessing each other minutely.

It's OK to be really businesslike and strategic in creating and organizing your various dating opportunities – you've got to do this to get anywhere. But once you're on the date it is best to try and let go and just enjoy discovering about one another – but only up to a point. To throw all caution to the winds is foolishness.

L♡vebyte

66 *Man*: Hey baby, what's your sign?
Woman: Do not enter! 99
Anon

A certain amount of strategy and skill is needed if you are to play your cards right and end up in a relationship rather than on a one-night stand – unless that's what you're after. So, how do you survive to date another day? To answer this question let's look at the dating strategies of some women I've met who are now in wonderful relationships – and who had a ball along the way! As we'll see, their behaviour and tactics are quite distinct from those of the women whose dates don't follow through.

The Domino Dating Strategy – put it into action!

Remember **Domino Dating**? To recap, as long as a man is at least 'friendship material', by dating him again you can set up a ripple, or Domino Effect which multiplies your opportunities. It's highly possible that one of the men you make friends with like this will become more than just a friend – simply because that's how it so often happens. But if it doesn't, then maybe some of the networking possibilities he can open up for you will be fruitful. The bottom line is: don't worry whether you fancy him or not; just ask yourself, 'Is he a fun human being and would I enjoy another hour of his company in the future?'

Win-win dates for you!

What *is* the recipe for success? We have already seen that you *can* organize the lead up to the date and the date itself in such a way that it is more likely to go well and go on to further meetings. But when it comes to the actual date, two people who are an ideal match may meet up and get absolutely nowhere. Alternatively, if they handle the situation differently, the same couple may well fall for each other. To put it bluntly, there are good and bad ways of setting the scene – and it's taken me many years of listening to feedback and doing informal research amongst my members to learn what they are. Mostly, they're a matter of common sense, but you'd be surprised at how few people really do themselves justice when they first meet an interesting person. As a result, instead of taking off, the date is just a damp squib. The rest of this chapter covers some of the easy-to-change date disrupters.

Smart phone tactics

If you have been introduced through an introduction agency, a personal ad, a friend or the internet, your first conversation may not be face -to- face but on the phone. You really need to be aware of the effect of your voice and your phone manner because vocal impressions can lead to snap judgements – just as first visual ones often do. A detailed treatise on the answerphone follows because this little box of tricks is *the* top saboteur of first dates.

SMART BIOG: **Did Sam give June a fair hearing?**

Let me tell you, first, about June and Sam. June was a friend to whom I'd given free agency membership. She was a PR officer for a charity and Sam ran his own software publishing business. I suggested a meeting but, when Sam rang June, he got through to her answerphone and heard what he thought was rather a flat, bored message – so he hung up. He had decided that she was not for him and formed a mental image of someone who worked in a tax office or funeral parlour. There was no fun, no warmth or energy there, he said. Alas, there was nothing I could do to persuade him to the contrary. She was attractive, great fun and had a good sense of humour, and I was *sure* they'd get on. He, however, insisted that he could *always* judge someone by their voice.

Being the interfering person I am, I managed to arrange for the two to bump into each other the following month at one of our social evenings. At first neither of them realized who the other was – and, yes, they got on like a house on fire. An hour later, I could see them still chatting and laughing together at a table in the corner. By this time, Sam had twigged what was going on, but June never knew she'd been rejected at the outset because she sounded flat and boring. 'In the flesh', her voice was warm and interesting; unfortunately, she hadn't bothered to ensure that her answerphone message reflected this. Sam and June went on to date regularly and have now been married for several years.

Your answerphone – friend or foe?

How, then, do you make sure your answerphone is scoring winners, not own goals? You can't avoid using this off-putting piece of equipment altogether, so make sure it's behaving properly and gives a cordial welcome to callers. I learned early on that, unless you're careful, answerphones give out lots of false negatives. The sound of someone's voice is a very potent force; yet, when people record an outgoing message, they are often in a hurry or are disorientated by unfamiliar technology – and the result is something that would frighten the horses! Put your outgoing message to the test now. Evaluate it critically. Does it sound 'pleased' that the caller has rung? Does it sound friendly and interesting, or is it too businesslike, moody or bored? Were you bending over the machine when you recorded the message? If so, that might be why it sounds 'throttled'?

This may seem like a lot of fuss, but do bear in mind that the smallest clues about you will be pounced on. All sorts of fantasies – both negative and positive – will be projected onto them and will influence the caller's response.

The answerphone reject list includes:

♡ **Background music – it's far too pretentious; who do you think you are? A radio presenter?**

♡ **Your child's voice – I appreciate that any future partner will eventually have to accept little Johnny and that they might as well get used to him from the start. The problem is that there may not be a start. It's wiser not to push the children to the front of the picture until you've built up some basis for a relationship.**

Always choose a relaxed moment to record your message. Centre yourself. Don't bend over. Stand or sit straight, take a deep breath and smile – yes, smile before you start talking into the mike. This way you will come across as open and friendly. Now, I know some of you use your home telephone number for work and that you can't, therefore, sound too informal; however, there's nothing wrong with sounding friendly and positive, even when wearing your professional hat.

You're ringing him – should you leave a message or not?

So much for your outgoing message, but suppose you are ringing him? If his number has been given to you by an introduction agency or he's responded to your personal ad, what about leaving a message on his answerphone? Because answerphones can so easily spike potential romances, I suggest to all our agency members that it's best to avoid leaving a message. The reason is that men and women relate to machine messages in totally opposite ways.

Women think nothing of treating anyone's answerphone like a best friend and have few inhibitions about leaving and answering messages. Most men, on the other hand, seem to be genetically programmed not to listen to their machines, even though they leave them on. As for returning messages – well, forget it. Furthermore, when he doesn't call you back after you have left a message, it starts to become difficult. If he does actually *listen* (!!!) to the several further messages that you subsequently leave, he may feel pressured by their insistence – no matter how much he'd probably enjoy meeting you. So, don't judge a man solely on the basis of his ability to reply to phone messages. When you actually meet him, you can then decide whether or not he merits the status of 'worth getting to know better'.

Persevere with your calls until he answers 'in the flesh' – and don't leave a message, but do remember to dial 141 (in the UK) first to ensure that your number doesn't show up dozens of times on his caller display; otherwise, he'll be confirmed in his fantasy fear that you're a desperate, man-eating, dragon woman! Reconcile yourself to playing lots of telephone tag. Busy, popular people are *very* difficult to get hold of. It's also sensible to avoid letting him know your terrestrial number till you are sure you can trust him.

Are you surprised by this description of men and telephones? Not all men are like this, of course, but as you don't know what you're dealing with at this early stage, play safe.

What do you say when you call him first?

He's written or phoned in a response to your ad in the personals and has given his phone number, or you've been e-mailing each other via an Internet dating site, or a friend is introducing you. Should you call him? Go for it! What can you lose?

First, make sure you pick a moment when you're feeling good about life! Are you relaxed and rested? Never phone a potential date for the first time after a stressful day at the office unless you've given yourself plenty of time to wind down. Have you been giving yourself some **TREATS**?

Once again, remember first to dial the code that prevents your number being revealed to him – just to be careful. As soon as he answers in person, *smile* into space (to ensure your voice is warm), say who you are and *immediately* check if it's a good moment for him to talk. He may be rushing off, late for an appointment, or have the lodger or children within earshot. All of this can make for a very abrupt and one-sided conversation, leaving you certain that he's not interested.

Now you're actually talking – great! Keep the call short if you already know something about him (via his letter, his introduction-agency profile or the friend who introduced you) – and keep it light. Don't try too hard to get to know one another over the phone – instead save your valuable small talk to break the ice on the date itself. Asking too many questions can come across as interrogation. Wait until you meet because then you'll be more spontaneous – with plenty of topics left to talk about.

Whenever I hear that a couple's first phone conversation lasted half the night (and this does happen), my heart sinks. The enthusiasm and euphoria of having encountered a kindred spirit builds up such huge expectations that the physical meeting is invariably a let down.

L♡vebyte

❝ Dating is a social engagement with the threat of sex at its conclusion. ❞
PJ O'Rourke

Should you initiate the date?

It's very difficult being a man and always being expected to take the initiative. If he sounds interesting, but doesn't get to the point and suggest a date during the first phone conversation – do it yourself. After a short but positive chat, try: 'What about a drink together next weekend?' Never say 'Shall we meet up sometime?' It's too vague and you're leaving it to him to make the decision.

Remember that dateworthy, successful people often have very full diaries, so don't be put off if you can't meet soon. But, arrange it *now*, even if the date is to be three weeks hence. Your goal, remember, if you're a **Domino Dater**, is to go out on as many dates as possible to give you dating practice and networking opportunities.

You won't sound pushy using these strategies if your mode is light, flirty and upbeat; so, before you get on that phone, read the next Chapter to learn how to be exactly that!

A 'date' or a 'drink'?

A first date, whether you're 18 or 80, is *different*. It's precisely because it is special that you need to plan a bit, even if it's only to ensure that you don't make it *appear* too special. Low key and flirty is the essence. In fact, many British males are so sensitive to the idea that you might have serious designs on them from Day One that I suggest you *never actually use the term* 'date'. If you are taking the bull by the horns and initiating a date, use Hugh Grant-like, non-threatening language: 'Um, what about a *drink* next Friday.'

For how long should you meet?

Be clear beforehand that you can't meet for long. My Golden Rule, remember, is that a first date should last a maximum of 90 minutes. Then, if you're panting to get away, there's no embarrassment because your date already knows that you won't be staying long. 'I promised to drop by and see my sister' or 'I've got to e-mail the copy to my paper by 11.00' should do the trick. If you don't fix the duration *before* you meet then it will be difficult to cut it short (without being rude), if he proves to be of no interest. Even if everything is going well, it is still wise not to meet for long. That way, you'll still have some easy conversation left for next time.

Long first dates are open to all sorts of pitfalls. Although you may be made for each other, you may still find you've moved rather too fast into exploring deep, personal matters: why you broke up with your ex, for example, or what you are looking for in your future partner is the kind of topic that can press the button marked 'panic' in either of you.

Where to meet?

Think carefully about where to meet *before* you first talk, and be ready to suggest several venues that you feel comfortable about. There's nothing worse than fumbling uselessly in your organizer for the address of that bar somewhere near the art gallery and then, for lack of planning, ending up agreeing to one that's miles away from where you live. Believe me, you'll feel distinctly resentful if you have to make three changes of train or a two-hour drive.

Avoid dinner dates and movies

For a first date, dinner is too long. First dates should be short. Keep to the 90-minute Golden Rule, even if you've booked the baby sitter and travelled hundreds of miles.

If you're meeting for a drink, perhaps after work, make sure it's at a place where you can also have a snack in case you're famished. Restaurants in the evening, however, definitely mean proper *dinner*, so choose somewhere more casual. A bar or brasserie is ideal. Pubs can be smoky, crowded and noisy and it's difficult to find a corner where you can talk without being overheard. If it's your style (and it's not everyone's), a hotel bar can be perfect: there tends to be more space and quiet and you won't have eavesdroppers all agog at the next table.

Some people swear by a weekend breakfast or lunch date because it's more fun and relaxed. If the weather is good, then a walk in the park, with afternoon tea at a café alfresco, might set the scene well.

An activity, such as a visit to an art exhibition, is excellent and provides stimulus for animated conversation – even if you don't know your Picasso from your Pissaro. Parties are not recommended as they may be too hectic for you to be able to concentrate on one another.

Avoid, too, going to a film, play or concert. You'll be sitting in silence, with an alien being sitting beside you, totally distracted from the performance as you speculate about how the two of you will get on once the show is over.

Personal safety checklist

For any woman who is meeting up with a man she doesn't know, there are certain common-sense safety precautions to observe. The more personal the introduction, the safer it's likely to be. If it was made through a personal introduction agency, for example, they will hold detailed records of all members and this is a powerful deterrent against bad behaviour. However, if your date comes to you by a more remote system, such as via an ad in the paper or the internet, you have much less control and need to be more vigilant. Although I've never heard of anyone having problems on the personal-safety front, it is always a theoretical possibility.

As I keep repeating, when you are meeting up with someone you don't know well, take care of yourself in the following ways:

♡ **Tell a friend where you are going and what time you are expected back. If there is no one appropriate to tell, leave a note with these details in a place where it could easily be found, such as in an envelope on your office desk.**

♡ **Always meet in a public place.**

♡ Don't meet in each other's homes till you feel you really know and trust the man.

♡ Always have your own transport home and don't accept a lift.

♡ If you find yourself concerned about your forthcoming meeting, get a friend to ring you on your mobile phone during the course of the date (apologizing profusely as, of course, it's bad manners not to switch your phone off). You can then indicate discreetly if everything is OK.

♡ Don't give your address to a man till you feel you really trust him. If he's even half-way decent, he'll understand and respect your wishes.

♡ Don't give out a terrestrial phone number to begin with. Your address can be traced from it.

♡ Always either dial the 141 barring code (UK) or use your mobile when phoning someone new. This will avoid your terrestrial number being traced.

I also recommend that you never agree to meet in the street – outside a station, for example. For some odd reason that I've never quite understood, couples from the agency who do this frequently don't recognize each other and both parties then ring us at the office furiously complaining that they've been stood up! However, as I write this, I have to hand a card from a member relating how she met the man she is seriously dating in front of a public lavatory – his choice! However, it was a posh, award-winning, state-of-the-art creation in a glamorous part of London.

Your ideal dating venues

Here's a nice, easy *Workout* – a practical one. Think of some venues you like that would make a good backdrop to your seductive powers and note your reasons for choosing them.

Mansearch Workout – My ideal dating venues

My list of congenial, relaxed dating venues and why I like them:

Venue   Why good for dating?

1) ....

2) ....

3) ....

4) ....

5) ....

Going on a first date
Overcoming first date nerves

Even though you're socially skilled and could, without batting an eyelid, chair
a conference for captains of industry or heads of state, meeting someone for
a first date may make your knees turn to jelly. An effective way of dispelling
nerves is to admit to them! Own up straightaway, 'I felt a bit scared on my way
here to meet you!' and your date will thankfully admit, 'So did I!' You'll both
laugh and any tension will be defused. It works. Try it.

The art of seductive conversation

To fascinate your man, you don't have to be the greatest wit that ever walked
the face of the earth. You can have him hanging on your every word if you
learn to engage in **proactive listening**. Forget the clichéd stuff about women
being 'good listeners'; it's not in this passive sense of the phrase that I mean.
Proactive listening is the technique of 'reflecting back' what your companion
says or feels – for instance, 'Obviously you really *enjoy* scuba diving'. This sort
of response shows you can relate to his *feelings*. If you also want him to feel
you've *understood* him properly, try 'checking out' what he's saying by para-
phrasing the essence of it back to him.

L♡vebyte

" Of flirting: Attention without intention. **"**

Anon

Be mischievous, flirty – and say what you think

I've already referred you on to the next chapter, which is all about flirting, and suggested you read it before making your first-date-winning phone call. Flip through it again before embarking on your first date. For now, though, the main thing to remember is that a date should be fun, upbeat and light-hearted – no matter what he's like. Jokey, teasing, mischievous, original and outrageous are all great. The art of flirting lies in being playful, curious and making you and your date feel just wonderful. However, don't be *too* eager, so he still feels there's some thrill in the chase. Crude, dirty or sleazy is out – and if *he* doesn't realize this, tell him.

L♡vebyte

" I wasn't being fresh with my hands. I was trying to guess her weight. **"**

WC Fields

Can't think of what to say?

Well, what *do* you talk about? It's easy to chat about the simple things that make up your everyday life: job, family, lifestyle, music, films, TV, sport, culture and so on – small talk rather than serious talk. All the interests and likes that you have in common, or that are complementary to each other, can keep you communicating right the way through the first date. A well-timed compliment can work wonders, even if it's just 'You look as if you're enjoying yourself' or 'Great tie!'

You also may want to get some indication about what makes the man tick: his values and beliefs, for example, or whether politics, current affairs or religion are important concerns for him. What does he think about some of the pressing issues of today, whether it's the future of the Middle East or the rain forests? Some men wouldn't be seen for dust if these topics arose, in which case maybe stick to favourite TV programmes.

Before going on a date, always scan the newspapers to be sure you know something interesting about what's going on in the world. Acquaint yourself with at least one political story and throw in something quirky, too. It never hurts to be up to speed on celebrity gossip. If you've no time to buy the papers, use the internet to read them – you'll find many useful 30-second digests of what's happening.

Reinforce your message

It's not so much *what* you talk about as *how*. Back up your 'soundbytes' with lots of eye contact, that's always a stunner. To make a real connection, make sure you say his name from time to time. There is a beguiling resonance in the sound of one's name being uttered by a relative stranger in an intimate context.

Furthermore, keep up the proactive listening: keep on reflecting back his words – at least until you're got into the swing of things. Once you've relaxed, you'll have no problem speaking your mind on anything that arises.

Subjects to avoid like the plague

A first date is much too soon to start talking about either your life goals or your emotional history. Be warned: you tackle such emotionally sensitive issues this early on at your peril! Even a couple of months down the line might be too soon. I do realize that it may be very tempting to bring up matters that are critically important to you at the outset, and thus avoid wasting your time on someone who might run a mile when you 'announce' them later. However, you do need to be sure that the other person is ready to share these issues with you before you bring them up.

L♡vebyte

❝ I require only three things in a man. He must be handsome, ruthless and stupid. ❞
Dorothy Parker

SMART BIOG: Gerald's painful divorce

I remember Gerald who'd had an acrimonious divorce and, as a result, had only very limited access to his children. He'd thought that at last he was ready to accept the situation and start dating again. He had a good response to his mail-out through the agency. On his very first date with Kerry, she asked him why he'd joined up. It seemed only natural to respond with a brief account of his divorce. Before two sentences were out of his mouth, the friendly smile was wiped off his face and he launched into the lengthy tale of his fight to achieve better access to his two young sons. The smile also fell from Kerry's face at this response to her innocent question, and a chill descended upon the evening. What was to have been a light-hearted and perhaps flirtatious chat had turned into a lengthy and heavy diatribe against Gerald's ex-wife. The date fizzled out and no mention was made by either of the evening being enjoyable, nor was there any suggestion of a further meeting.

SMART BIOG: **Rashida's baby deadline**

Here is another example, and this one happens all the time (women with bio-clocks running out – please note). On their first date, Rashida told Jerry that she wanted children before she was 40 (only 18 months off). Jerry told me that, in spite of wanting children himself, he started to sweat profusely and simply couldn't keep the conversation going. They didn't see each other again.

Small talk before 'big talk'

The lesson from these unsuccessful first dates is that you *can't* take short cuts in the process of getting to know someone. Talking about anything emotion-ally intimate, such as why you broke up with your ex, is *fatal*. Any un-addressed resentment or unfinished business will be obvious to your date. Remember, too, that men and women often have different timetables for deal-ing with intense or painful matters.

L♡vebyte

❝ If at first you don't succeed, try, try again. Then quit. No use being a damn fool about it. ❞
WC Fields

It is important in any relationship to understand how your companion is coming to terms with past situations. On a date, you can get a lot of clues from their body language – for example, for outward signs of reticence or defensiveness. There is a section on body language later in this chapter (see pages 137–39).

If your date is the one who talks about why he broke up with his ex, tell him that you read somewhere that couples who discuss such matters on early dates usually don't see each other again. Say 'Tell me, instead, how you feel about ...' and mention another topic you can both discuss safely. Focus on questions that are likely to elicit a positive rather than a negative response. The more you can encourage your date to get into 'Yes' mode the more likely he is to feel good about you and to want to see you again.

A smart answer to a tricky first-date question

What if your date starts to interrogate you about lots of personal details that you don't feel ready to discuss? Try responding with 'I'll pass on that one' or 'Ask me in a few weeks'. Providing you say this firmly and with good humour, he should get the message.

Talking time

People often talk too much when they're nervous and may take over the conversation, thus giving the impression that they're egotistical, arrogant and boring. Observe the conversational flow, and note whether one of you is doing more talking than the other. It could be you but, guess what? It's usually the man who monopolizes the airwaves and the woman who colludes with him by listening begrudgingly and passively.

L♡vebyte

❝ When it comes to making love, a girl can always listen so much faster than a man can talk. ❞
Helen Rowland

There is well-documented research that shows that men do tend to talk far more than they realize. They are more likely to do this in stressful situations – such as on a first date – and it may not be truly characteristic of the normal run of their life. If you're ever in this predicament, with a man rabbiting on endlessly about his job at the bank or his passion for fly fishing, try and snap him out of it with something like, 'Hey, half time! – I'd like to tell you about me now.' Back it up with a smile, a friendly touch on the arm and a bit of direct eye contact and he'll be all ears. You can rehearse this one at work or in any social setting where you are not getting your share of the stage. Remember that a person who talks too much can't do so unless he or she has a colluding audience.

Reading the hidden agendas – body language

What does he really think about you? Is he wildly attracted to you – or is he dying for the date to end? Tune in to a man's body language and you'll get useful feedback on that first date. We all know about defensive arm folding, but it may be more difficult to tell whether his fidgeting is to do with nervousness or the fact he can't wait to escape. If he's stroking the rounded vase on the table, is this sensuousness or is he bored? Is he leaning towards you showing interest in what you're saying, or is his gaze wandering? Is he genuinely smiling at you, or is it a bit forced and 'glazed'?

There is no sure-fire translation of body language, but you can usually draw accurate conclusions if you're observant and it's a subject well worth studying. In Chapter 3, I suggested that scrutinizing the body language of a potential date was a good way to assess your next moves and recommended one of the best books I've found on the subject: *Body Language – How to Read Other's Thoughts by Their Gestures* by Allan Pease. It makes fascinating reading.

The body bares all!

How is your body speaking to him? What messages are you giving out? Are you smiling – but not too much? Are you showing appreciation – but not too eagerly? Are you maintaining appropriate eye contact? Make sure you are sending out the right messages and not falling back into those old, off-putting habits such as holding your hand in front of your mouth when you speak, or offering a wet-lettuce handshake!

Mirroring his body language can be an important way of connecting. See if he mirrors yours in any way. What is he consciously or unconsciously trying to tell you? In the 'Mirroring Body Talk' section in Chapter 8, (see page 164) you will learn what an important role this plays in disarming the nervous defences of the man you're with, and in upping the level of 'electric' voltage that you need in order to move in to 'super flirting'.

All parts of our bodies are actively involved in 'communicating' our thoughts and feelings. Here are a few examples of messages you can pick up from the hands and the head. Are any of these characteristic of you? If so, are they giving out a wrong message? If you see any one of these in your date, ask yourself if they are telling you something you need to know. On the other hand, they could be part of his charm!

When the hand is supporting the head

We often do this when sitting down, propping up our chin in our hand with our elbow braced against a table or the desk. It usually indicates that we are tired or bored. If the hand strays around over the face – maybe covering (and thus hiding and protecting) the mouth – then this is very probably a signal of anxiety or nervousness. The less confident we are feeling, the more our hands tend to be on the move.

Hands clasped behind the head

If a person is standing with their arms flung open – or lolling back in a chair – with hands clasped behind the head, this is a sign of someone who is feeling very at ease, and confident enough to expose that most vital and vulnerable of organs – the heart. It is often used by people (especially men) comfortable with, and revelling in, their authority. However, both men and women may also lean back in this position when savouring a job well done.

Hair patting and grooming

When someone is constantly patting and adjusting their hair, it is an obvious sign that they are preoccupied with their appearance. They may be anxious about it – or just plain vain. If they are unconsciously fiddling with their hair and pushing it back from their forehead, this may be unconscious preening – a courting signal. Women will often season this with some head-tossing.

Hair twisting

Hair twisting can reveal a lot of nervousness. Women tend to twist their hair more than men do – possibly because they have more of it. It's a tremendous give-away to bosses and people interviewing you. It is also easily read by your date.

Running the fingers through the hair

Running your fingers through someone else's hair may be extremely romantic. Running it through your own tends to indicate exasperation, frustration, anger or even despair. Of course, there may be a more mundane reason if your date is doing it. He could simply be trying to ensure his bald patch is covered!

Fingers touching the mouth

Nail or finger biting, however fleeting, can give out a negative message. It is often a sign of insecurity or anxiety. When children suck their thumbs, they are regressing to their mother's breast or the feeding bottle. Touching the mouth may help us feel more centred, but it can be off-putting to the observer. We may grow to love a characteristic gesture like this in a loved one – but first impressions count for a lot.

Touching the neck

A hand moving up to touch or rub the neck can indicate that your date is feeling very uncomfortable. The discomfort may derive from the fact that they are lying! If they clasp the back of their neck (assuming it isn't stiff from the draught of an open window or from playing squash), they may unconsciously be expressing anger. Noting this, you may be able to avert it.

Tugging at the collar

Another nervous 'clue' can be someone running their fingers around their collar, or trying to pull it away from their neck as the heat of anxiety or tension rises up towards the head. It is a gesture often made by someone on the brink of a 'big' moment, such as a bridegroom awaiting the bride. Fiddling with the collar can also indicate embarrassment or even guilt; you'll often have seen this when a politician or an official rises to make an evasive speech.

And now who pays?

At the agency, we always recommend that both people offer to share the bill. However, I think that if the man really wants to pay, let him. It's a bit of old-fashioned courtesy and should never be treated as if it were a put-down. If you know there's going to be another meeting, you can always say, 'My turn next time'.

Finishing a date when you want to see him again

You've enjoyed yourself ... a couple of drinks ... some small talk to break the ice ... and then chatting in a relaxed way about each other. Is there a bit of a spark? Yes, but you don't know yet if there's any real chemistry. Being a Domino Dater, you decide you should see more of him. In which case, it's time to part while you have still got lots more to discover about one another. In the old days, the man would say at the end of such a date 'That was great – most enjoyable. I'll give you a ring sometime.' Then, he might or might not have got back to you. Even nowadays, if he doesn't keep his promise and you'd really like to see him again, you may still feel that you are supposed to be waiting for him to take the initiative, and be reluctant to call yourself.

The problem lies in a striking and basic difference between men and women – and one already mentioned in relation to answerphones. For a woman, it's the most natural and easy thing in the world to pick up a phone and call someone. For many men, it's neither easy nor natural. The fact that he said he'd call you, but didn't do it promptly, makes him feel guilty and compounds his inaction, even though he might really like to see you again.

Smart endings to promising first dates

At the agency, we cunningly suggest that women should take the initiative in rounding off a promising first date with a man in one of the following ways:

You finish the date sooner than he expects

The date's going well. You'd like to see him again. Keep him on his toes by getting in first and saying something like, 'I enjoyed that, but I've got to go now. Maybe we could give each other a call in a week or two?' This implies that any further initiative is evenly shared, and thus the man won't feel pursued if you, the woman, ring him and suggest another (low key) date.

Many women do feel hesitant about phoning a man. However, our feedback from men is that they *love* to be rung and invited out by a woman *unless* it had been arranged that man would do the phoning – in which case he feels pressured if the woman calls first. This is why, at the end of a date, it's so important to ensure that *either one of you* might call the other. If you phone him when he said he'd call you, you'll appear emotionally needy. In fact, if you do anything to imply that the relationship is more serious for you than him – he'll run a mile!

The whole issue of who rings whom is a tricky one. This is because, on the one hand, you want to play just a teeny bit 'hard to get' to 'keep 'em keen', while, on the other hand, you're dying for him to chase you. It helps to be not too predictable about your phone calls or availability and also to drop clues about *seeing lots of people at the moment*, 'just as friends', of course – so they don't think you're sleeping around. Manipulative? Yes, maybe, but opt out of this strategic dating completely and you'll be the loser. But if you become too strategic, as the best-selling dating book *The Rules* advocates, you'll be pretending to be someone you're not. He will then fall in love with a false personality – not yours.

At last, I've reluctantly mentioned *The Rules*, by Ellen Fein and Sherrie Schneider, which advocates NEVER calling a man and NEVER accepting a Saturday date if he asks you after Wednesday! NEVER have sex unless he promises to marry you. To be totally like this, you'd have to be frigid, calculating – and ghastly – but the consensus amongst the women I've questioned is that it's fine to use these tactics, say, *10% of the time* to keep him on his toes. That's quite reasonable, I think, and certainly works a treat.

Get him to say 'yes' to a second date on the spot

However, what about those brilliant dates where it's obvious you should see each other again and it would be churlish just to say you'll ring each other rather than fixing something on the spot? Which of these two invitations is more likely to elicit a second date?

'I really enjoyed meeting you. Shall we meet up again sometime?'

or

'I really enjoyed meeting you. Are you free, by any chance, to meet for another drink, say next Wednesday or Friday?

Obvious isn't it? Be specific, but give alternative dates to choose from. Of course, he can always refuse, pleading another engagement, but at least you are in with more of a chance than if you'd been vague and non-specific about the invitation. Too forward? It depends on how you do it. Providing it's a low-key date, suggested in a humorous, no-big-deal manner, he'll be delighted. However, only try this approach if you are confident of a positive response.

You leave the door open – in case you want to see him again

If you're not sure whether you want to see him again, keep your options open. In our experience at the agency, at least half the couples who do form a relationship were uncertain, after the first date, about whether there had been any chemistry.

The best way to judge the success of the date is not by trying to guess whether you could spend the rest of your life in the arms of this man, or even to try and determine whether you could have an affair. Remember, you're a Domino Dater. Just consider whether he'd be fun to meet and talk with again. Could he be a friend? From this viewpoint, you can get to know several men as friends and see how things develop. The chances are that one of these could turn into something special, or could lead to another introduction that *is* the one for you. Play the field, go for volume and meet as many men as possible. When you meet the right one, you'll be in good practice for giving out positive messages and be more likely to judge the situation accurately. If previously you've been on only a few dates, you'll be much less able to judge the potential.

Providing, on every date, you make it clear that you're seeing other men, it's fine to explore multiple friendships. The more time you take to get to know one another before the chemistry ignites (and not just the sexual tinder), the more powerful and enduring all that follows will be.

If in any doubt, leave the possibility of a further meeting on the back burner. You can simply use the old standby: 'Maybe one of us can give the other a ring in a week or two'. It does, in fact, take the pressure off men to know that you're not expecting anything too dramatic at this early stage. They are perpetually concerned that they'll be thought to be 'leading a woman on' and then getting lumbered with all sorts of expectations that they can't live up to. Rather than risk this, they'll play it too cool and not ring at all – so leave the door open.

You don't want to see him again – so you're kind but clear

If you have the certain feeling that you don't want a second date, you can chicken out by letting the man say 'I'll give you a ring sometime' and then tell him you're busy when he does. Personally, I think it's much better to be clear at the outset while at the same time being sensitive to your date's feelings. Thank him for taking the trouble to meet you, and say you've enjoyed talking with him, but you don't feel you want to take it any further for the moment as you're seeing lots of people. You can always add that, if it's alright with him, you'd like to keep his number in case you have a friend who'd like to meet him. Agency members, including the men, say they much prefer this more honest approach because they know where they stand. However, this has to be done with unpatronizing sensitivity.

L♡vebyte

“ *Man:* I'd like to see you again. What's your number?
Woman: It's in the phone book.
Man: But I don't know your name.
Woman: That's in there too. **”**

Should you kiss on the first date?

You're tempted to kiss on the first date because he's gorgeous and you know he wants it too. I'm talking about a real snog here, not just the polite peck on the cheek. Should you? The smart solution for the woman looking for a real relationship rather than a one-night stand is to remember that instant passion is easy, but the slower and more tantalizing the build up to that first kiss, the more exciting it will be and the more likely it will develop into something special. I say keep him waiting and stick to subtle language. To create high-wattage sexual electricity, give him a taste of sensual delights to come by going for the 'brushing' kiss – cheek-to-cheek or mouth to cheek and extend it for that electric split second longer to whet his appetite and keep him wondering. Please note, I didn't say mouth to mouth!

If, on the other hand you do think he's attractive, but just want to keep your options open, give a quick combined mini-hug and cheek-to-cheek kiss which is friendly and yet not over-intimate. Stick to an arm squeeze or an amiable handshake if you are unsure where you stand or if you don't want to see him again.

'OK', I can hear you say, 'but what if he lunges at you and starts a French kiss on a first date and it's a case of "yuk" as you're not keen or not ready?' Not an easy one! I asked a lot of women about this and most would reject the kiss by backing off. Some were so embarrassed on the occasions this had happened that afterwards they avoided eye contact and decided on the spot never to see the man again. If he's a drunken lout – that's fair enough. Supposing, though, that he's a really nice, sensitive, nervous guy who's terrified of first dates and simply has no sense of what's appropriate? Being an assertive Domino Dater, you want to try and avoid cringe-worthy incidents and feel you've handled the situation to the best of your ability. So practise this response: push him away firmly, establish eye contact and say, 'I'm not ready for this – I need to know a man really well first.' There can be no rule about kissing. Let's face it, every situation must be judged individually.

L♡vebyte

 " It wouldn't be a good idea
 To let him stay.
 When they knew each other better –
 Not today.
 But she put on her new black knickers
 Anyway. **"**
 Wendy Cope from 'June to December 1: Prelude'

Leaping into bed

You ended up between the sheets on the first date. It was the second bottle of Chardonnay that did it, on an empty stomach (you were obviously sticking to my advice about avoiding dinner on first dates). You can't adhere to good sense all the time. It happens – we've all done it. And if you know he's someone you can trust (not someone you know nothing about), who am I to say anything about lust for lust's sake?

The problem arises when feelings are sparked off which seem to be more than just lust and you wake up in the morning dreaming about buying the three-piece suite with him or what you're going to name 'our' children. Then you may have jeopardized a future relationship by getting too close too soon – if things become too emotional early on, you won't see him for dust.

L♡vebyte

" I want to tell you this terrific story about oral contraception.
I asked this girl to sleep with me and she said 'No'. "
Woody Allen

On the other hand, never let yourself be pressured into sex if you're not ready for it. Just say, 'Hold on, I feel great about you, but give me more time'. Be a little hard to get. It allows space for the relationship to develop at a tempo that suits both of you.

Safe sex? Well, I assume you're wised up on this one, so I'll say no more than 'Always be prepared'.

You fancy him like mad – but he doesn't feel the same

It always hurts. Rejection is part of the dating game. Accept that a percentage of dates won't want to take things any further. Thank him for coming and wish him well. Be a good loser. There are plenty of more heavenly men around – now that you know you can find them. You're only after *one* special one, anyway. See the end of each chapter for ideas on how to pick yourself up when you are feeling low. Organize those TREATS.

First-date mistakes

Try this Workout and learn from your own experience:

Mansearch Workout – What not to do on a first date

The great date that didn't follow through. Why not?:

1) ....

2) ....

3) ....

4) ....

5) ....

What have you learned from this about changing your tactics? (Make a note of your conclusions.) Maybe you were:

♡ too effusive;

♡ too keen;

♡ too cool;

♡ not cool enough;

♡ too passive;

♡ too tired;

♡ in a venue which was too noisy;

♡ short of conversation;

♡ drinking too much;

♡ talking about the wrong things;

♡ feeling distracted by work worries;

♡ feeling disappointed.

To ensure that everything goes well on your first date, the following Keynotes & Diary Prompts summarizes the do's and don'ts:

Keynotes & Diary Prompts

DON'T

1 Leave messages on answerphones. Persevere till you can speak *personally* to your man.
2 Meet for longer than 90 minutes – the Golden Rule – on a first date. End the date leaving lots more to discover about each other and keep him panting.
3 Talk about:
    ♡ your therapy sessions;
    ♡ your ex;
    ♡ wanting to have children.
4 Drink too much.
5 Talk on your mobile phone.
6 Appear too desperate or needy.
7 Say, 'I'll give you a call sometime' when you don't mean it. Be honest but kind and sensitive about rejection.
8 Expect to be able to judge your date's relationship potential on a first date. If you could be 'just friends', try and see him again. Remember the Domino Dating Strategy!

DO

1 Ensure your answerphone is man-friendly.
2 Always meet in a public place.
3 Dispel nervousness by owning up to it.
4 Ask lots of questions without being too nosy.
5 Practise the art of reflective listening.
6 Use your date's name in conversation.
7 Use a lot of eye-contact.
8 Find something about him to compliment.

9 Be polite – to the waiter too.

10 Always offer to split the bill.

11 Always have your own transport home. Politely refuse a lift.

12 Follow the personal safety code.

13 Have fun! Relax and enjoy yourself!

By now you are probably better equipped than anyone you know to turn a first date with an interesting man into a second date. But to be sure, that you don't lose sight of the fundamentals, tackle the next **Relationship Action Plan** and then reward yourself with the mandatory **TREAT!**

RELATIONSHIP ACTION PLAN 7

Note down your Smart Action points for the next week.

Positive Action 1:

....

....

Positive Action 2:

....

....

Positive Action 3:

....

....

Treats

Before you read Chapter 8, do something that's a treat just for you. For example:

♡ Make an *aphrodisiac snack supper*: wine, olives, avocados, delicious bread, smoked salmon, paté, prawns, rocket and radicchio leaves, tomato and basil salad, peaches, fresh figs, chocolate mousse, mango sorbet, Turkish delight. (Well, perhaps not all of them!)

♡ Make a date with your Diary to acquire, preferably in the next week, one *item of clothing that makes you look and feel really slinky and sexy* – it can be designer label or charity shop.

♡ Book yourself in for *a good manicure, pedicure or facial* – or all three!

Louise began to have second thoughts about the Advanced Flirting class her friend had recommended.

chapter 8

Turn Men On and Pull Them In

The flirting gene

'Help! I'm not a born flirt', I can hear some of you say. Wrong. You *were* born a fabulous flirt. We were *all* born fabulous flirts. Psychologists believe that flirting skills are hard-wired into the human species. Since the Stone Age, we have instinctively flirted to help us identify and attract the most likely mates for successful breeding and care of the resulting offspring.

Nowadays, however, flirting is not just a vital means of identifying your best bet for a partner, it's also a basic form of communication between people in any social setting. It simply goes into a higher gear in romantic and sexual situations. The good news is that you can develop this innate flirting ability to a state-of-the-art level. I'll show you how you can do this with aplomb.

First, though, we need to get something sorted out. Isn't flirting all about being a manipulative coquette, being fluffy and getting round men? That's not the philosophy of the independent, 21st-century female, surely? So, what are the meanings attached to this often misused term?

The conventions of coquetry

I remember my grandmother telling me how a 'lady' could make herself more desirable to a 'gentleman'. Before appearing she should take a gentle breath and silently articulate the word 'brush', which should leave her lips enticingly parted so that they were like 'the petals of a new rose just bursting into bloom.'

L♡vebyte

" Modesty: the gentle art of enhancing your charm by pretending not to be
aware of it. "
Oliver Herford

This glorious strategy was, I suspect, one among many listed in Victorian books
on charm and etiquette for attracting the attentions of men. Visual signals,
accessories and metaphors of dress were used to communicate *indirectly*
with the object of your interest. The fan lent itself to a whole language of
flirtation. (Actually, I've always had a sneaky suspicion it was invented to mask
gusts of bad breath emanating from mossy fangs – the result of poor dental
hygiene).

Flirting has been associated both with the demure heroines of Jane Austen
novels and the thrusting breasts and pouting lips of Hollywood sex sirens: from
the barely expressed through to the most brazenly explicit. What's going on?
The dictionary defines flirting in many ways – most of them implying superficial
or pretend courtship. For example: *'To try to attract sexually without serious
intent'*; and *'One who pays or invites attention merely for amusement.'*

L♡vebyte

" A lady's imagination is very rapid; it jumps from admiration to love, from
love to matrimony, in a moment. "
Jane Austen, Mr Darcy in *Pride and Prejudice*

The modern minx

However, these dictionary definitions do little justice either to the complexity
of flirting or to its positive role in everyday life today. Flirting has become
respectable and professionals – for instance, those in the communication business – regard it as a powerful tool of persuasion as well as a means of turning
up the hormonal voltage when required.

Using the next Mansearch Checklist , check out where you are right now with
the idea of flirting. What has it meant for you?

Mansearch Checklist – What does flirting mean to you?

Tick one or more of the following:

Sexiness   ☐
Manipulation   ☐
Friendship   ☐
Tartiness   ☐
Attraction   ☐
Teasing   ☐
Hypocrisy   ☐
Fun and games   ☐
Feeling good   ☐
Duplicity   ☐
Seduction   ☐
Irresistibility   ☐
Chat up   ☐
Other meanings: ☐

....

....

It will be interesting to see whether you chose positive or negative definitions of flirting. What do your answers say about your upbringing? Do you see any of these flirt styles as being your particular hallmark or ambition?

Release your inner superflirt

We know that small babies learn early on that smiling and cooing bring about positive attention. In the same way, adult flirts use their skill to bring about desired outcomes, but for many of us, our original childish flirtatiousness was actively discouraged throughout our youth. Our culture tends to discourage flirtatious behaviour and smother the natural impulse to flirt. So, how can you get more in touch with your innate flirtatiousness? First, by having heaps of fun doing the Workouts in this chapter – starting today! Then, flex and flaunt your flirt muscles by setting up lots of positive dating situations. This way you can explore different ways of getting in touch with the inner, more flirtatious – and deeply attractive – you.

Learning to become fabulously flirtatious is definitely *not* about 'grafting on' new gestures and behaviour, but about feeling so wonderful in yourself that you want to share this with another person and make them feel great, too. It's something we can all tune into, providing we throw all our inhibitions to the wind and create plenty of positive flirt feelings – and situations in which we can practise them. But maybe you still harbour some resistance to flirting – like Ann ...

SMART BIOG: 'Wouldn't flirt, even if I could!'

'I've no time for flirting. Game playing and manipulation – that's not my style.' I can still hear the echo of Ann's vehement protests that day in my office when I pointed out that the feedback from her dates was that she was far too serious. 'Wait!' I said to her. 'Before you write off a highly potent, partner-pulling asset, think again.' I suggested that exploited and repressed women of times gone by frequently needed to use indirect, manipulative flirting techniques to gain access to love, favours and, indeed, their means of survival. The women of this millennium, however, can be far more direct and up-front about flirtation because of their greater independence and confidence.

'But I haven't got a flirtatious gene in my body', Ann remonstrated, 'I wouldn't know where to begin.' I spent an hour persuading her and, after some gasps of horror, she apprehensively agreed to go on a weekend flirting course run by my friend Peta Heskell, a professional flirt coach (yes, really). There, she could learn to connect with her inborn flirting ability and do light-hearted and practical role-plays in a supportive group.

After the weekend, Ann dropped by and said that she hadn't had so much fun for years. There had been some interesting people in the group and she had really enjoyed the flirt role-plays. She felt excited because she was starting to see dating as being a delightful adventure rather than a necessary means to an end, and it was with enthusiasm that she selected a dozen men to whom the agency would send her profile and photo.

That was years ago. The event slipped out of my mind until recently when a woman came in to join up and mentioned that she had been recommended by 'Ann and her husband Bruce' who had met through us and had had twins two years back. They sent their love ...

Game, set – and match?

Flirting today in Western culture is more likely to be between two equals *who both know it's a game* – and one they gleefully engage in. The less socially powerful woman of the past had, of necessity, to play the game for real – and win – in order to ensnare the man who would be her provider.

L♡vebyte

❝ I live by a man's code, designed to fit a man's world, yet at the same time I never forgot that a woman's first job is to choose the right shade of lipstick. ❞
Carole Lombard

Now, flirting has moved on; but, thank goodness, 'game-playing', in the modern, more positive sense of 'being playful', is still at the core of flirtatiousness. For example, playing just a little 'hard to get' and the 'thrill of the chase' can generate amazing erotic electricity. Sexy flirting is more about teasing and tantalizing than manipulating someone's feelings. Nevertheless, as with any communication technique, flirting can be misused. The price to be paid for exploiting it is that you may end up attracting the *wrong* men.

'Hot' flirt role models

An excellent way of getting into flirt mode is to summon up the image of a successful seductress whose methods appeal to you. To help identify suitable flirt role models, consider the personalities in this next Mansearch Checklist. Whose flirt style would you most like to emulate? You may be more inspired by women from your own circle of friends, or public or fictional characters. If so, add their names to the list.

Mansearch Checklist – My favourite flirt styles

Tick one or more of the following:

Renée Zellweger ☐
Kim Catrall ☐
Shilpa Shetty
Sara Jessica Parker ☐
Kylie Minogue ☐
Gwyneth Paltrow ☐
Madonna ☐
Nigella Lawson ☐
Jennifer Lopez ☐
Sarah Harding ☐
Cheryl Cole ☐
Carla Bruni ☐
Michelle Obama ☐
Penelope Cruz ☐
Angelina Jolie ☐
Jennifer Aniston ☐
Oprah Winfrey ☐
Other examples – friends, fictional characters, etc: ☐

....

....

Let's look at why the first 'flirt role model' you chose is so special. Try this light-hearted Mansearch Checklist to get some clues.

Mansearch Checklist – My No. 1 flirt role model

Tick one or more of the following adjectives to describe your ideal flirt style:

Naughty ☐
Sexy ☐
Sizzling ☐
Playful ☐
Wicked ☐
Witty ☐
Friendly ☐
Demure ☐
Cheeky ☐
Clever ☐
Smouldering ☐
Other adjectives: ☐

....

....

With practice you'll be able to select, almost unconsciously, the style of flirt-ing that best suits your personality and is appropriate to the occasion; so, let's get down to some basics.

Friendly flirting and sexy flirting

Nowadays, flirting is seen as being about much, much more than just dating and seduction. It's part of the ongoing business of communicating in any social con-text – be that among strangers or work colleagues, men or women. So it makes sense to think about it as two separate but overlapping types of behaviour – friendly flirting and sexy flirting. 'Nice day, isn't it?' said to the receptionist or postman with a spontaneous smile, is friendly flirting. Sexy flirting is, of course, about communicating desire and lust for a man you *seriously fancy*. It's when you sensuously tousle your hair with one hand while holding his gaze for that electric split second longer than is expected. It's when you tease and tantalize his sexual appetite.

L♡vebyte

❝ When a woman wears a low-cut gown, what does she expect you to do:
look or not look? ❞
William Feather

With the person you eventually grow to love, friendly flirting and sexy flirting
merge and are about nurturing the relationship through all its stages – from your
first night of unbridled passion through, hopefully, to your naughty nineties.

Flirt your way to work satisfaction

Flirting in the broader, more friendly sense is something that earns promotion
at work, too. The women who all the men in the agency want to date are also
noticeably more successful and happy in their careers than those who don't
attract so much interest. To succeed at being a good boss or colleague, in the
normal run of things, means you *have* to have the flirt factor. Aggression and
manipulation don't score many points in the workplace. Being interested in
and sensitive to others' needs (in addition to one's own) certainly do.

All-inclusive flirting

Of course, it's not just about being flirty with the opposite sex, but with the
same sex, too. Women whom men find attractive are also charming, funny and
flirty in the company of women. You don't have to be a man to respond to a
flirtatious and charming woman. At the agency interviews, our female consultants not only can tune into female applicants' friendly flirting, but can easily
spot those who'll shine at sexy flirting.

L♡vebyte

❝ When I'm good, I'm very, very good, but when I'm bad I'm better. ❞
Mae West

It seems as if, for today's woman, success with the opposite sex isn't just about
fluttering her eyelashes or playing coy. She's got to be charming, fun, confident and considerate with all sorts of people, not just the man she's interested
in. And, last but not least, happy with her own sexuality.

Nurturing the flirt factor

Flirting is infectious and can be sparked off by the right context and people. I've seen many people blossom as flirts as a result of being around encouraging, happy, flirtatious people and putting themselves in positive situations. This enables them to be more in touch with the 'child within' and feel playful and curious – all essential pre-requisites of being able to flirt.

Many new women members of the agency say that starting to date again, after a famine of men, can induce feelings of self-esteem and euphoria that catapult them into automatic flirt mode. Feeling good means feeling more attractive – and it shows! It's a self-fulfilling prophecy. Nevertheless, *you* still have to create the necessary opportunities.

SMART BIOG: **Tanya's story – leaving space to flirt**

Tanya, a solicitor in a legal advice centre, found that few of the first dates she went on resulted in a second date, even when she really fancied the man concerned. She was an attractive woman but, I learned, had lived on her own for five years and had been so busy with her work (about which she was passionate) that she had quite got out of the habit of dating. At the age of 38, she felt she was now ready to find a partner and settle down to start a family. The combination of being out of practice and the countdown on her bio-clock made her very focused – in the wrong sort of way. I heard from the men she met that she 'interrogated' them on their parenting aspirations more or less as if she were interviewing them for a job, the job of being her future partner and father of her children.

I knew from experience that a relationship was an unlikely outcome of this over-determined strategy. She was pretty devastated and also angry with us that things weren't working out the way she'd planned. To what extent should I interfere? This 'bio-clock syndrome', as we call it, sabotages the chances of many women in their late thirties and early forties. I suggested she come in and have a review session. When I told her about the feedback I'd had on her dates, she was silently reflective. I wasn't sure how she was taking it. Then, to my relief, she asked me what I thought she could do to improve matters.

After a lot of talking, we came up with a **Flirt Action Plan**. Tanya needed to do everything possible to create space to get into flirt mode instead of scaring off men by her determination to find a partner. We agreed that she would resign from a couple of her work-related committees so that she would have more time to relax, enjoy herself and see friends. When she went on a date, the plan was that she experienced it completely in the present and did not even consider her date's 'partner potential'. At first she found it difficult to let go of her 'headhunter' questions. I heard from the Agency consultants (who get all the feedback) that it was only after she had been on a number of further dates that she had started to relax and express her flirty side.

I got a card from her three months later – and guess what had happened? An ex from years past had reappeared and they fell in love all over again. Tanya later insisted that this would never have happened if I had not persuaded her to defocus and be less driven, both in her work and her partner search. This had helped to create the right preconditions for romance, even if it did come from an unexpected quarter.

L♡vebyte

" No self-made man ever did such a good job that some woman didn't want to make a few alterations. **"**
Frank McKinney (Kin) Hubbard

Switching on flirtatious feelings

Here are some powerful techniques you can learn to enhance your flirting ability. I am deeply indebted to Peta Heskell (some of whose ideas I have adapted here) whose book *The Flirt Coach* is essential reading for would-be great flirts.

Learning to flirt more effectively isn't just about learning new behaviour. First and foremost, it's about getting in touch with the golden, feel-good space deep down inside you without which it's impossible to flirt. You can think of this as a 'pre-flirt mode'. How can you get into this 'pre-flirt mode' at times when you're feeling really nervous and inhibited? It's the same technique that athletes use to get into 'winning mode' before a big event. To get them into peak performance mode they try to recreate the positive feelings related to previous occasions when they have won. By imagining the sounds, sights, smells, feelings and excitement surrounding the occasion, they become empowered.

The 'Golden Glow' of success

You, of course, are not trying to win – just trying to flex those flirt muscles. Do it now. Shut your eyes for a minute and conjure up the feelings associated with a moment in your past, a golden moment, maybe in your childhood, when you were deliriously happy, relaxed, curious, wondrous and playful – in a **Golden Glow**. Try and identify all the sensory elements that make up this memory. What did you hear, feel, touch, smell or taste? Imagine the scene as a film starring yourself. Intensify the colours. Enlarge the picture. Put yourself right in there.

Lock on to this Golden Glow and let it flow through your body. Where do you feel it? Your throat perhaps, or maybe your belly? Describe it. Is it like the warm rays of spring sunshine? Feel the smile spreading across your face.

Finger on the flirt trigger and ...

To evoke this Golden Glow at will, and get yourself into 'pre-flirt mode', you need to link it to a 'trigger'. Choose a special gesture you can make, such as wiggling your toes, or scratching the end of your middle finger with your thumbnail. Do it right now! Repeat the gesture and generate the Golden Glow until you have created an association between the Golden Glow and your personal **flirt trigger** so that, any time you want to flirt, you simply 'fire' your trigger. This way, you can evoke the feelings directly and can quickly slip into a fabulously relaxed state that enables you to float effortlessly into flirt mode.

Practise this technique several times a day until you are able to conjure up this Golden Glow at will by using your trigger – or even without it. Now, you're ready to get into flirt mode – whether it's to be in an everyday friendly encounter or a romantic one. The secret is never to think 'I must flirt right now. I MUST FLIRT'. This is an absolute killer. You won't be able to flirt. Instead, think 'Hey, I want to connect a bit more with this person', then trigger your flirt mode and enjoy yourself.

Some people also find it helpful to visualize the image of their flirt role model. They visualize their voice, their body language and conjure up a picture of this person flirting. Then they imagine they *are* that person. Try practising this one too: really believe you *are* Kim Cattrall, Renée Zellweger – or that friend who hoovers up the men at every party. Now you're ready for some practical flirting pointers.

Everyday flirting

If you are great at friendly flirting, remember: it's only one gear-shift up to being a stunning, sexy flirt! So practise your friendly flirting at every opportunity. You can check out which everyday flirting situations you need to brush up on by tackling this Workout.

Mansearch Workout – Brushing up your friendly flirting skills

If you feel that people are less friendly these days, then practise:

♡ Opening conversations with strangers – it's an opportunity to extend your horizons.

If you clam up when the conversation runs dry, then practise:

♡ Asking people to expand on an earlier point they made.
♡ Asking what they think about a comment you made earlier.

If you run out of ice breakers when you meet someone new, then practise:

♡ Building up a repertoire of openers, especially compliments, and use it with all sorts of people – in the post office or at the gym.

If you feel it's much easier to talk to women than men, then practise:

♡ Exploring a friendship with a man who may be interesting but not obvious relationship material.
♡ Stick to friendly rather than sexy flirting.
♡ Be prepared for things to change and for any new opportunities that may emerge from the situation.

These are all well-tried communication techniques that will help in any type of friendly flirting context. At the bus stop tomorrow try 'Ohmigod! Three buses in a row' or 'Can I say hello to your dog?' Avoid serious topics and stick to everyday stuff like this. In the corner shop try 'Busy today?' or 'Cold, isn't it?' Try to get into the habit of giving more compliments to friends and work colleagues. You'll make their day – and yours. Flirting is not about impressing people with conversational content; it's about establishing rapport and making connections. But don't forget to trigger and connect with those relaxed, happy Golden Glow feelings first, so that your flirting comes from the heart.

L♡vebyte

** If you are flattering a woman, it pays to be a little more subtle. You don't have to bother with men, they believe any compliment automatically. **
Alan Ayckbourn, *Round and Round the Garden*

To ensure your flirtatious feelings are translated into flirtatious action, try these simple techniques:

The low-down on flirty talk

Proactive listening

Don't listen passively when in conversation with people. Practise reflecting back their feelings and views to show you are empathizing with them, for instance: 'So you're really into wine tasting ...', or 'Working as a teacher must be so demanding'. Proactive listening also provides you with hooks for attaching your own ideas.

What's in a name?

Actually saying the person's name while conversing with them is a very powerful way of establishing a bond. Simply: 'By the way, Stephen ...' will do the trick. Nowadays most businesses instruct their staff to identify themselves immediately on answering your telephone call. You can get into the daily habit of using people's names by saying, 'Thank you Janet/John' every time you phone a company or directory enquiries. It establishes immediate rapport.

Compliments

Compliments are sure-fire winners. With friendly flirting, go for compliments and flattery about clothing, jokes, stories, etc. For amorous and sexy flirting, take it further. If you know you really fancy them AND you're confident of some sort of reciprocity, use 'body talk' for more personal compliments. Hold back on sexy compliments, though, till you're sure they'll be welcome and that you mean them. You don't want to seem too eager – or be done for harassment.

Mirroring body talk

The effective flirt appreciates the value of subtlety and realizes that body language speaks more powerfully than words in many romantic situations. Mirror any of his positive body language and you'll disarm his defences, as any sales person will tell you. If he lowers his voice and talks more slowly – you do the same. If he inclines his head towards you – do the same. Lean on your elbows if that's what he's doing. Return a direct gaze – it's electric. See how much more *you* feel in tune with him. *He* will feel the same about you.

Sexy electricity – upping the voltage

When you want to generate more sexual electricity, cast your mind back to how you felt the last time you were truly attracted to someone. That feeling of sexy excitement can easily be rekindled. First, use the technique you've been using to get into basic flirt mode, and conjure up that relaxed Golden Glow throughout your body. Then, to feel really sexy, imagine the last time you were really turned on! Recall what you saw, heard, smelt and felt at the time – the electric exchange of glances, sexy compliments, romantic music, the smell of aftershave and that frisson of excitement.

L♡vebyte

" Lead me not into temptation. I can find the way myself. **"**
Rita Mae Brown

As with evoking the 'pre-flirt mode', suggested earlier, practise associating these memories with a chosen flirt trigger (such as caressing your ear lobe) to anchor the memory so that you can trigger it at will. Do this now and hold on to this heightened sensation of sexiness, letting it pulse through your being. Even imagine it has a colour and move it around your body to really experience the sexy sensation.

If you prefer, you can picture yourself as (for example) Halle Berry emerging from the sea in the James Bond film *To Die Another Day* – aware of her sexuality and flaunting it one thousand per cent.

L♡vebyte

❝ I knew right away Rock Hudson was gay when he did not fall in love with me. ❞

Gina Lollobrigida

Now you're ready to practise some sexy body language.

Teasers to try

Your smile

By far the most commonly used part of your flirt repertoire is your smile. But don't smile all the time – it looks as if you're desperate to be liked. An effective smile is used sparingly, on its own, as a statement or to reinforce other messages. Let it suffuse your face after a moment's reflection in response to something your date has said or done.

The glance

A glance establishes rapport immediately. It signifies that the two of you are on-line and ready to send messages, either verbal or non-verbal. The merest flicker of a glance can speak volumes. Blended with barely raised eyebrows and a Mona Lisa smile, it can raise blood pressure a notch or two.

The gaze

The intensity of the message is revealed by the gaze, whether it says, 'I'd like to know you better' across a crowded room at a party or, 'I fancy you like crazy – let's make love'. There are few gestures more charged with sexy electricity than prolonged eye contact.

The sideways glance

A sideways glance is very sexy and will disable a man's defences before he realizes he's been disarmed. This piece of body talk is particularly effective if emanating from behind a curtain of tousled tresses nonchalantly flung back mid-glance.

The wink

Only wink when the electricity is sizzling and if you're the cheeky type. Go easy, it needs to be no more than an imperceptible flicker of an eyelid, almost so that he wonders if he imagined it. Less is more.

Your voice

Your voice may be the very first impression he has of you. In Chapter 7, in relation to answerphones (*see* pages 125–6), we explored the fact that a harsh, nasal, high-pitched or monotonous phone voice can zap your chances before you've even met your quarry. On the other hand, a warm and winsome voice can make up for all sorts of shortcomings in other areas. Your voice *is* something you can work on with great results. Tape your side of the next phone conversation and listen to it critically. Bad posture and breathing together with nervous tension are probably the biggest culprits responsible for poor voice delivery. For immediate improvement – whether on the phone or 'live' – centre and steady yourself, breathe naturally, and consciously relax while speaking.

An investment in sessions with a voice trainer can give you a kick-start if you think there's a problem, and you can fine-tune an already good voice with stunning effect. Politicians, VIPs and actors do this all the time, knowing full well that their voice is one of their most valuable assets. However, effective voice production requires determination and can take a while – so think medium-to-long term. Whatever you do, don't ignore your voice! It can be one of your most potent weapons of seduction as well as something that will take you far professionally.

Even more tactile messages

When you're into sexy flirting, touch enters into its own. Sensuously caress your hair; play with your necklace or earring, twirl your cocktail stirrer (or whatever other small object is to hand) and you give out powerful sexual signals. But, note well: do it slowly with just enough provocation to suggest what you're getting at. Don't tackle it in a way that makes you look as if you've got a premature attack of Parkinson's or you might as well go home.

Kiss me quick?

Whether to kiss on the mouth on a first date is a question that often comes up in discussions (see the previous chapter). I would say that the answer is no, particularly if you hope the relationship will take off. The slower the start, and the more time you give to discovering one another, the better. The good flirt who fancies a man will be giving out all sorts of subtle clues that it will be well worth waiting for any kind of intimacy.

Rejection? – their loss!

As your success rate in any endeavour increases – so will your failure rate. It's part of the risk. Be prepared for rejection when you practise friendly or sexy flirting and you'll learn to pick yourself up afterwards and be a good loser. Be brave and don't let it put you off opening up further connections.

L♡vebyte

❝ She wore too much rouge last night and not quite enough clothes; that is always a sign of despair in a woman. ❞
Oscar Wilde

Remember that you'll never find out which people in this world around you are interesting unless you communicate with them. As a rule of thumb I say that, out of every five first dates, two will be rejections, one will be a bore, two could become good friends and, after following the advice in this chapter, one of these two could be that special person. Keep thinking: 'There are plenty more fish in the sea' because, for organized, proactive women prepared to be adventurous – there are! If things don't turn out the way you hope with your drop-dead gorgeous date, it's ... NEXT PLEASE!

Flirting and the Domino Dating Effect

By now you will have realized that the Domino Dating Effect is central to learning new flirt skills. By aiming to date as many men as possible, you create a ripple of even more dates – really useful flirt practice and you meet other interesting men in the process. These are the perfect conditions for practice in triggering your flirt mode and for trying out your flirt skills. Furthermore, one of these interesting men may turn out to be that someone special! You can even practise on the no-hopers – BUT keep the boundaries absolutely clear between friendly and sexy flirting so that you don't mislead anyone.

Flirting with the no-hopers?

In Chapter 7, we looked at that first date you just know you don't want to date again. But even if he's the least likely Mr Right, remember it's only a date! He still deserves all your best friendly flirting attentions. He has given up his time to meet you. Be kind and charming without any hint of sexy innuendo. Be clear from the start that you're seeing lots of other men and that you don't want to second date any of them – just at the moment.

Busting flirt blockers

Are you still finding this flirting business a bit tricky? The next Mansearch Workout will help you to resolve various common obstacles to fruitful flirting:

Mansearch Workout – Busting flirt blockers

If you find it difficult to flirt when the man you're with only talks about himself, then practice:

♡ A few conversation turners using good eye contact, saying his name and a light touch on the forearm to reinforce your message. Remember, first date anxiety propels many of us into nervous behaviour.

If you go into a huff when a man rejects your flirtatious advances, then practise:

♡ Picking yourself up without putting the person down and just move on to the next opportunity.

If you suspect that you're sometimes too effusive and go over the top when trying out flirting techniques, then practise:

♡ Watching people's body language for signals; for example, drawing/turning away from you, tightening of lips, reduction of eye contact, narrowing of eyelids, tone of voice changing.

If you tend to look away when an attractive man gazes at you, then practise:

♡ Triggering your flirt mode, then holding that eye contact for a couple of seconds to maintain the electricity – and offering a smile.

If you wait for that sexy man at the party to make the first move, then practise:

♡ Making eye contact with him and going over to say, 'Hello, can I join you?' Don't forget to smile and trigger your flirt mode as you do this.

If you never seem to find men attractive enough to flirt with, then practise:

♡ Flirting with anyone who is interesting and nice. Sexy electricity is not always immediately evident and may only manifest itself in your quarry in response to your flirt signals. If the situation doesn't develop – well, his brother might be the man of your dreams or he might offer you a business contract.

Your Wow! Factors

OK. Flexing those flirt muscles will help you captivate some wonderful man, but what about those special personal characteristics that will boost your attractiveness? Let's call them 'Wow!' factors. Can you identify any of your underused Wow! factors – those that will now benefit from unleashing with the help of your new-found flirt skills? Being aware of unused potential has to come before you can develop it – and then it can change your life!

What are these female qualities that truly have the men weak at the knees? To check this one out, I thought it would be interesting to see at the agency whether the women who men found attractive were just great flirts or were there other common denominators underpinning the attraction? We looked at the women who all the men wanted to date and tried to see what exactly made them distinctive – what gave the Wow! factor.

When the men were asked by our agency consultants to describe the woman they'd be *seriously* attracted to, certain attributes appeared on every shopping list. We then checked to see if these attributes tallied with those possessed by the women the men *actually* selected and wanted to see for a second date. The popular women had oodles more in common than they had differences, and we'll see that the Wow! factor isn't always long legs and swishy hair.

What men said they wanted

These are the characteristics the men said they were looking for in a woman for a life partner:

♡ Confidence;

♡ Optimism;

♡ Independence;

♡ Curiosity;

♡ Sense of humour;

♡ Physical attractiveness (yes, this one really does come after the others when the men tell the consultants what they want – but we suspect political correctness is the reason they don't put it first!).

All this was what the men *said* they sought but, in the real world, perhaps, coquettes, vamps and bimbos still hold sway no matter what they're like as people or how much men protest to the contrary. So let's see ...

The women who Wowed!

It was simple to verify whether the men meant what they said about the women they found attractive. At a staff meeting, we looked more closely at those women whom nearly every man wanted a second date with. What were they like? The consultants looked at their notes. Yes, of course, the **physically attractive** women got a lot of initial attention, but it didn't always translate into a second date. And yes, you'd describe the popular women as having **sex appeal** – although, interestingly, this is rarely mentioned by the men, I think it's just assumed.

The women who all the men wanted to second-date were all much more than just sexy and physically attractive. They were:

♡ **optimistic;**

♡ **relaxed;**

♡ **confident;**

♡ **direct;**

♡ **kind.**

They were also:

♡ **humorous;**

♡ **fun –** *even* **playful;**

♡ **approachable;**

♡ **friendly.**

A 34-year-old architect, Charlie, summed it up for me: 'With Alison, what you see is what you get – she's a really happy soul with a great sense of humour. We broke your 90-minute first-date rule, Mary, and talked till they threw us out of the wine bar, and we've planned to meet up again next Friday.'

Powerful women – do they really scare men?

We find that most women believe men are scared off by power and high earning capacity in a woman, no matter how much of the Wow! factor she possesses. We discovered this is not really true – providing she is not aggressive in the sense of trying to come out as top dog. Rob, a 41-year-old accountant, put it in a nutshell: 'Sue, what a personality! I can see why she's a barrister – imagine her in court! I fell for her not only because she's an independent, ballsy woman, but also because she's not any kind of put-down artist.' We find that, *providing* she's **kind** and **sensitive** about other people's feelings, a powerful personality in a woman (as in a man) is a bonus in the attractiveness stakes. What about women who earn more than their dates? This is not usually a problem for the men unless it means a big gap in lifestyle and spending patterns. So please, all you women captains of industry, don't say to me that men are scared of you. Providing you're not the ball-crushing type, then strength and power definitely pull aplenty.

L♡vebyte

❝ No woman marries for money; they are clever enough, before marrying a millionaire, to fall in love with him first. ❞
Cesare Pavese, *The Business of Living: Diaries* (1935–50)

Flirt boosters

It's time to start tuning into the more flirtatious you – right now. To ensure that you are well and truly in flirt mode when you need to be, check out some of the following flirt helpers to boost your confidence and your chances. Flirting is theatre. You need the atmosphere, the backdrop, the props, the smells (especially perfume) and the costumes. Never underestimate their importance. Let's look at some of these.

Setting the scene

Whether we're talking restaurants or bedrooms, check that the atmosphere is conducive to your plans. If it is to be a restaurant or bar, avoid noisy modern venues full of brushed aluminium and ear-splitting music – hopeless for having an intimate conversation. Gentle atmospheric lighting, rather than piercing spots, will show you at your best. Make sure the tables are not too close so you don't feel inhibited in your conversation. Selecting the best venue will help both of you relax and be yourselves. In your own home, the same goes for lighting – and don't forget room temperature, music, some flowers and a good tidy-up.

Dress to flirt

Ignore clothes at your peril. I know you may feel you don't want to graft a false image onto yourself, but you *can* be YOU and still look a million dollars. Wear something you know you look great in. Figure flattering is a must, but, apart from this, anything goes – from trainers and jeans to elegant attire and designer labels, as long as you look and feel good and it's appropriate for the venue. If in doubt, it's always best to dress down slightly for a date; overdressed and you'll give the impression of bothering too much, and this might make you look needy.

L♡vebyte

❝ Some people are born with a sense of how to clothe themselves, others acquire it, others look as if their clothes had been thrust upon them. ❞
Saki

In Chapter 6 we looked at many of the things that we know men find off-putting. These can include bulky clothing, scarves, jangly jewellery, pearls and obvious make-up. Blue, green or pearly eyeshadows are definitely out (they are ageing); so is gooey lipstick. If you wear eyeliner, make sure any hard edges are softened to a smudge with kohl pencil. Remember, too, that men also dislike very short hair, so avoid an urchin cut unless you are an 18-year-old gamine type – even if your well-meaning friends swear it suits you!

High on the list of handicaps for women, at least on a first date, are specs. Once a man gets to know you, they don't seem to matter; but first impressions do count here. Yes, I know it's unfair, and men don't seem to suffer from the same specs prejudice from women; but this book is about how it *is* in the dating game, not how it *ought to be*. If you do wear specs, remember to turn them – sexily – to your advantage. Use them as a flirting prop, rather than a barrier, by removing them from time to time to reveal your eyes directly – to tantalize and tempt.

If you are on the slightly plump side, we find that it's best to opt for flattering, dark, rich colours and give white and pastels a miss. Avoid tent-like dresses or anything too tight. Buy clothes that fit you and never wear a top and bottom of a different colour. Remember, jerseys and cardigans make us all look at least a size bigger than we really are. High necks can give the impression that your breasts start under your chin – go for V necks wearing them as low as you dare.

Flirting for foodies

Ah! The shared enjoyment of food and drink is great flirting foreplay. Cooking together, especially with a beer or glass of wine in hand, offers a gem-on-a-plate opportunity for communing, relaxing, sharing, warmth, sociability, sensuality and flirting. You don't need to have seen Nigella Lawson, 'Ready, Steady, Cook' or the seductive interplay between Albert Finney and Diane Cilento over that sexy supper in the classic film *Tom Jones* to know how outrageously seductive food can be.

There is something about the candlelit dinner – low lights, delicious food and fine wine – that never fails to put one in the mood for romance. However, beware of talking with your mouth full and watch out for that bit of spinach that always gets between your front teeth. I've glued a small handbag mirror just inside the cupboard door over my kitchen sink – which is perfect for discreet tooth inspections and has saved me from many an embarrassing moment as I smilingly present the dessert.

Aphrodisiacs – seductive morsels!

I nearly forgot about aphrodisiacs! If you want to serve a-tongue-in-cheek (literally) Valentine dinner, you *must* feature some of the following:

Tomato and basil salad – The tomato, once called the 'pomme d'amour', was introduced by the Spanish and banned by the Puritans as morally dangerous. The basil is for its sensuous fragrance.

Oysters – They tantalize with their sexy taste and appearance – and are full of zinc for fertility.

Asparagus – Their phallic shape is to be delicately savoured and sensuously licked.

Truffles – Fungi that are found under oak trees, are worth their weight in gold and have an aroma, pungently redolent of sex. Shaved into a lightly tossed omelette, they're irresistible.

Mangoes for dessert – Shared between you in a warm, perfumed bath – the only place to eat this fruit at any time.

Belgian chocolates – Contain phenelethylamine, a chemical that flows through the bloodstream when you make love.

A sense of humour – Surveys show this is one of the biggest aphrodisiacs. What's more, it's free and a lot easier to get hold of than rhino horn or Spanish Fly!

The only other comment I would make on the sexy-food scenario is: 'Watch out for the onions', so that your love-making climax isn't accompanied by a drum roll!

Fresh air and exercise

Another classic preamble to seduction and flirtation. It seems that those feel-good endorphin hormones really get buzzing after exercise and fresh air in the country.

On our profile form at the agency, we have a question about what would be a 'perfect day'. Although they know it's a well-worn cliché, a large percentage of our members still own that, for them, a country walk, followed by a delicious meal or maybe a massage in front of a log fire, is the perfect prelude to a romantic evening. Of course, this is more of a city dweller's fantasy and is, probably, rarely indulged in; but the idea is great.

We all know the feeling of relaxation after a good stride out in 'the sticks' followed by a drink in a country pub. Some of our townies insist that the endorphin 'hit' is just as high – and therefore equally conducive to romantic interludes – after you both do a gym session or play tennis. You know what puts *you* in the mood, so make it happen more often!

'If music be the food of love ...'

It's not for nothing that those Elizabethan courtiers were always playing the lute and singing madrigals, but you must tune into music that your flirtee can relate to. Check out sounds that you both like and let them set the scene. Just ensure that your choices are romantic and stimulating without being intrusive.

Flirtatious messages

Little notes just saying: 'Hi, thought you'd enjoy this', with some diverting article, a CD, a book review or perhaps an apt cartoon, can be great flirt aids – friendly or sexy. With sexy flirting, e-mails and text messaging are the modern versions of the old-fashioned love letter and can send many hearts a-flutter. Also, between friends and work colleagues, this form of informal messaging, perhaps mentioning the latest snippet of gossip, does much to oil the wheels of sociability. There are many sites with free e-mail greetings cards. However, beware of what you send to people's work e-mail addresses or fax machines because bosses and colleagues may have access to them and you don't want to cause them any embarrassment.

Answering machines

Answering-machine messages can be used to great effect in the flirt stakes providing you know they won't be overheard by the nosy cleaner, some spotty teenager or, heaven forbid, the ex who's over on babysitting duty. They offer much scope for mischievous and risqué flirting, but you need to be sure of your ground and what sort of sense of humour your man has or you could be getting the brush off quicker than you can say 'first date'. (For more on answerphones, *see* pages 125–6.)

Texting

Fantastic flirters know that texting and sending pictures via your mobile phone is great for spontaneous and rapid fire communication. Texting is so user-friendly that you can easily risk over-exposure. Remember not to come across as too available and thus send the flirtee into panic mode.

Growing attraction

The suggestions in this chapter have worked for many other women and they can for you too. Commit yourself to getting out there, on some interesting dates, with anyone who's roughly right, and practise turning up your attractiveness voltage. You don't want to risk dating any toads? Hold on a minute – remember Domino Dating? Every date sets up that ripple effect – and ripples can lead to great waves. It's only by going out with some of the wrong men that you learn to recognize the right ones.

You only need a few fun practice dates to start being more mischievous, dazzling and curious. And if you're not enjoying yourself, fake it till you feel it. To be more relaxed about flirting, spice up your week with lots of those little, friendly flirt opportunities. Don't forget to trigger your flirt mode first. These everyday flirt moments are the building blocks for becoming a sizzling, sexy flirt.

And now, to ensure you're using every gram of your inner attractiveness and flirtatiousness, tackle your Keynotes & Diary Prompts, your Relationship Action Plan and then – your well-earned TREATS:

Keynotes & Diary Prompts

1 Feel good about YOU. As in any learning situation, the happier and more positive you feel the better. Refuse to encourage any tendency you have to be depressed or stressed out. This will hamper your chances of romance with the right person.
2 Re-read the section in this chapter about how to anchor a personal 'trigger' to connect you with that deep-down, euphoric Golden Glow. This will ready you for radiating flirtatiousness whether in a friendly or a potentially sexy situation.
3 To learn any new behaviour, you need to practise and practise again to hone your new skills till they become unconscious and automatic – so create lots of opportunities for friendly and sexy flirting practice.
4 Increase your flirting expertise by associating with good flirts and modelling their behaviour. Don't forget to become a flirt-watcher – observe others flirting and become more aware of how they operate.
5 Next time you walk down the street, experiment with gaining attention – not as a flamboyant exercise, but through the subtle use of beautiful body language. Let it resonate in every movement.

6 When you're next in a crowd, make eye contact with at least three people. Tell them something with your eyes – even if it's only 'I like your socks'!

7 Cultivate all those can't-do-without flirt-helpers – your clothes, haircut, make-up, accessories and, of course, the stage management of timing, venue, lighting, music, food, drink.

8 Think of someone you really fancy – in real life, or a celebrity. If you were going to flirt with them, what six things would you – could you – do to catch and hold their attention. Imagine this as a fantasy situation where everything goes perfectly.

RELATIONSHIP ACTION PLAN 8

Note down your Smart Action points for the next week.

Positive Action 1:
....
....

Positive Action 2:
....
....

Positive Action 3:
....
....

Treats

Before you read the next chapter, write down in your Diary what your next batch of TREATS will be. For instance:

♡ *Light a candle when you take your bath.* If it's a broad (fat!) candle, put a couple of drops of your favourite essential oil around the wick – as well as in your bath.

♡ *Buy some flowers on your way to work* (what colour do you need today?) and put them where you can see them throughout the day.

♡ Did you decide whether *a new-you perfume* was a good idea? Either way, book in your Diary a time when you'll head for a shop with a good range and do a sampling session – and, possibly, a buying session.

♡ While you're in the store, and giving the perfume samples a chance to 'settle in', see if there are other little TREATS shouting to you. How about a really *beautiful frame for a treasured photo?*

Alan and Clare recalled the sheer animal attraction of their first meeting.

chapter 9

How Will I Know When It's Love?

Falling in love – the chemical explosion

You are breathing faster, going hot, your heart is racing, butterflies are coloniz-ing every atom of your being. Your blood feels like liquid nitrogen, adrenaline is seething through your veins. Your pupils are dilated. You feel strangely disturbed. Your appetite diminishes. Exhilaration slips over into euphoria. To confound you with science, heightened emotions also release phenylethylamine, a chemical also found in chocolate, and occytocin, which surges forth when you even think of kissing or sex. Your friends tell you you're mad. What's behind this hormonal volcano? Drugs? No, it's 'just this thing called love'.

L♡vebyte

❝ Love is a fire. But whether it is going to warm your hearth
or burn your house down, you never can tell. ❞
Joan Crawford

Of poets, philosophers and scientists

But what is love? Are we to understand it as this transient high, or are we think-ing of a profound, lasting and tender happiness? It would be rash of me to attempt an ultimate definition of love; it means something different to each of us. Poets, philosophers and scientists have been struggling with the 'love enigma' for cen-turies because, despite all its commonly shared emotions, love arises from a unique relationship between two individuals. Today's cultural notions of love, however, can more easily be recognized than the scientific because they are obsessively repre-sented in the media, pop songs and movies – and they are powerfully sexual.

The most astonishing thing about modern ideas of love in the West is their diversity. In the more structured and hierarchical societies of the past, the way people understood love and beauty and the way they courted each other were bound by strict conventions. These behaviour modes varied, of course, within and between cultures and also according to social rank, religion and class. The ritual and complexities of medieval courtly love, for example, were very different from the rough and ready courtship of the average peasant.

L♡vebyte

" Love is a temporary insanity curable by marriage. "
Ambrose Bierce

Monroe to Madonna – images of love

Today, in the West, most of these social divisions have been broken down and we live in a common consumerist culture in which images of love, beauty and attractiveness are kaleidoscopic and constantly shifting. Nevertheless, we are all still driven to some extent by a set of common assumptions about what love is, often without being aware of it. Our grandparents were conditioned to a greater extent to the escapist clichés of Hollywood. In their day, a frequent model was the zany blonde and the tough guy making out – Jean Harlow and Clark Gable, for example, in the red-hot *Red Dust* (1932). Today's generation has been brought up on a wider spectrum of models and on a diet of greater social realism. TV shows such as 'Neighbours' and 'Sex and the City', and zesty icons as Madonna and Catherine Zeta Jones influence everyday ideas about love and romance. The pages of *Hello!* magazine reveal it all.

Yet, all these popular representations of love can create expectations that obstruct the forming of genuine loving relationships – unless, of course, you are sufficiently aware of how they impinge on you. This is because they relate to the initial phase of love or 'lovesickness' that usually fades after a couple of years. If you're lucky, it's replaced by a gentler, emotional intimacy that can last all of your life. If you're unfortunate, this initial phase of 'lovesickness' may collapse completely, prompting you to seek another and yet another fix. Sometimes the break is so painful that you're scared of exposing yourself to the torments of love again, and avoid further emotional intimacy.

L♡vebyte

" 1 Don't see him. Don't phone or write a letter.
2 The easy way: get to know him better. **"**
Wendy Cope, *Two Cures for Love* (1992)

L♡vebyte

" My wife and I thought we were in love but it turned out to be benign. **"**
Woody Allen

Recognizing true love

'How will I know if it's really love?' you'll ask yourself when contemplating a new relationship. The moment when eyes first meet across the room, the electric touch of an unfamiliar body, the first kiss – all seem so convincing every time. Each of us has our own idea of how to judge whether someone is potential partnership material. The more realistic your criteria, the more likely you are to form a happy, healthy relationship. How can you be sure, then, that it's the real thing this time around?

How, too, can you avoid repeating past mistakes, whether these relate to thinking it's love when it isn't, or not recognizing love potential when it's handed to you on a plate? Clearly, there is no all-purpose success formula for this process; but at the agency we do notice that certain types of people are more likely to get it right – the ones who are more realistic. Others have a tendency to wander into a romantic cul-de-sac – those who want *everything* on their Perfect Partner Shopping List.

Understanding why and how you tend to fall in love can help enormously in releasing the energy needed to overcome obstacles to your relationship goals. It's then easier to put positive strategies in their place, strategies that are more likely to work out for you. To help you understand your own pattern in more detail, complete the next Checklist. Simply decide if you have ever colluded with the following notions. Come on – own up!

Mansearch Checklist – Your beliefs about falling in love

Tick whether or not you agree with the following statements:

	Agree	Disagree
The one and only man for me is out there somewhere.	☐	☐
I'll know when I meet him if it's to be the real thing.	☐	☐
If there is something that irritates me about a man, then there's little chance he could be the right one for me.	☐	☐
If I'm not sexually attracted to a man at the beginning, I know it can never work.	☐	☐
I will be truly fulfilled when I find my life partner.	☐	☐
I just haven't met the right one yet.	☐	☐

And any other beliefs you have about falling in love:

....

....

How many of these statements apply to you? If there are three or more, then you need to question seriously your expectations about a relationship, if you are to find and create a happy and permanent one. This may sound brutal, but the most common excuses used by people for not being in a relationship are based on such myths.

The problem for some is that, even when they are ready to commit themselves, they have formed the habit of clutching at these powerful love myths. Let's look at these influences on your destiny and make sure they can no longer trip you up. Initially, the real reason for you not being in a relationship may be that you are not ready for one, or that you are blocking it for some psychological reason. Or perhaps you simply don't believe that it is possible for love to blossom from unlikely beginnings. Either way, a long trail of potential future partners is left by the wayside.

Love Myth No. 1 – That 'One and Only Special Person'

When you were young you dreamed of the moment when you'd find that 'One and Only Special Person', that 'One and Only Love', out there, waiting for you. Films, magazines and songs all connive with this myth. No matter how intelligent, how well educated, how successful you are, there is the likelihood that you will have been touched by it.

Is that 'One and Only Special Person' for you out there, lurking in the wings? Will it be the first man you meet or the tenth – and what if he's holed up in a monastery in Mount Athos? With this myth, every new love is compared to the ideal and found wanting in some way. If there is *anything* missing from the plot, you know it can't be right. Maybe he's been married before, maybe he already has children or perhaps he's shorter than you. You feel you must be short-changing yourself if he fails on even one count.

Dating addiction

The 'One and Only Special Person' myth, can have you leapfrogging from one serial date to another, always hoping the next one will be 'Him'. In other words you've become a 'dating addict'. So, although I advocate going on lots of dates before you make up your mind, beware of this pitfall. Dating addicts believe that relationships are found ready-packaged; they don't grasp that they need to be cultivated and flirted with even when all the signs are favourable. It's for this reason that we rarely let people stay in the agencies for more than two years in case they become what we call 'corn-flakes' or serial daters.

L♡vebyte

❝ When I was a young man I vowed never to marry till I found the ideal woman. Well, I found her – but alas, she was waiting for the ideal man. ❞
Robert Schumann

SMART BIOG: **Paula's holy grail**

Paula was a 27-year-old systems analyst who had been dating lots of men, but had never settled down with any of them for more than a couple of months. She believed that she would definitely 'know' when she stumbled on the 'One and Only Special Person' for her. She only had to meet enough men and she'd recognize him. He, too, would realize that she was the 'One and Only Special Person' for him. Sadly, it never worked out that way. Maybe our introduction agency could be the answer. 'I simply don't want to waste his time, or indeed mine, when I know he's not for me,' she protested when I questioned what looked suspiciously like a serial-dating habit.

Paula was young and having good fun. I suspected that she might not want a settled relationship yet; maybe the time wasn't right. Perhaps she was unconsciously using the 'One and Only Special Person' myth as a rationale for this – as so many people do when they just want to enjoy themselves. We discussed it. She was unsure and so we both felt she should pause and think about it for a month or two.

In fact, I didn't see Paula again for two years, after which, having sown her wild oats and failed to harvest them, she was ready for commitment and came to see me again. This time, I invited her to join up. The most heavily-emphasized item on the Action Plan that we drew up for her was that she cease to discard men after one date for failing to be instantly recognizable as the 'One' – somewhat hesitantly, she agreed. In this way, she could allow space for a different kind of relationship to blossom *and* something good to develop. It did when, six months later, she met Allan, an ear, nose and throat surgeon.

Everything had gone wrong on their first date. He was an hour late due to a hospital emergency ... she'd turned off her mobile phone ... he couldn't reach her ... she assumed she was being stood up. Added to all that, he was exactly her height and she wanted someone taller – so she could wear heels. She'd always gone for 'public school' and his accent suggested to her that he wasn't. When it came to paying for the drinks, he thought that she (being a modern woman) would be offended if he didn't let her pay half, and she felt that he ought to pay the lot.

Remembering her Action Plan, she somehow angled for a second date – which, to her surprise, went swimmingly – and, yes, they became an item and, as far as I know, they still are.

Cultivating Mr Right

There are, I maintain, many Mr Rights out there for every woman. It's crazy to think there's only one. In the agency, our observations have led us to the conviction that if you meet 20 men who are 'roughly right', the chances are that you could spend the rest of your life in a happy relationship with any two or three of them – *if* you are prepared to give all remotely possible introductions a chance to develop. In other words, follow my Domino Dating Strategy (*see* page 7).

The 'One and Only Special Person' myth has resulted in many lost opportunities. It also distracts us from understanding that relationships are created and not found. Because of the myth, very often little attempt is made to get to know someone beyond the first acquaintance unless they immediately pressed that Mr Right button. Considering what they had to live up to, on a stressful first date, their chances of doing that are very slim.

It is the ability to 'grow' a relationship that is the essential ingredient of success, other things being equal. Of course, values, outlook, interests and physical attraction are also important, but, for many people, letting go of the 'One and Only Special Person' myth can be a truly liberating achievement. Is this the myth that's sabotaging *your* chances of finding a partner?

L♡vebyte

66 We come to love not by finding a perfect person, but by learning to see an imperfect person perfectly. **99**

Anon

Love Myth No. 2 – 'I'll know when I meet him'

Jasmine was in a similar mould to Paula and had belonged to another introduction agency before she came to see me. She was one of the *'lightning will
strike me between the eyes'* brigade. She, too, believed that, if there wasn't
instant chemistry, it would never work. My heart sank as I guessed what she
was going to say about her experiences at her last agency.

SMART BIOG: Jasmine's 'wrong chemistry' formula

'I had a good time.' Jasmine proceeded to tell me, 'The agency was excellent.
I met someone new and interesting about every two weeks – mostly great
guys, successful and with lots to say for themselves. The dates were fun –
sometimes we talked for hours. It's true there were three or four with whom
I had loads in common but, no, there was *no real chemistry*. I didn't want to
lead them on. I've already got lots of friends with not enough time to see
them so there was no point in encouraging more. I simply didn't find them
sexually attractive and knew I never would. I thought I might stand a better
chance in your agency.'

Jasmine's problem was that she was confusing the *chemistry of raw, sexual
attraction* with the *chemistry of love*. Indeed, this sexual chemistry is
so potent that it can be spotted across a crowded room when two people
have clicked.

Fatal attraction?

John Cleese and Robin Skynner, in their book *Families and How to Survive
Them*, wrote about a fascinating experiment which shows how, even without
being allowed to talk, people in a crowd can be drawn by their body language
to others who have been raised in a similar emotional environment. It is this
instant recognition of a kindred spirit that can ring the fatal bell that
announces: 'He's the one for me'. Only children are drawn to other only children; offspring whose parents were divorced are attracted to others with a
similar experience; orphans to orphans, and so on. In other words, these people are speaking the same emotional language. Couple this with physical

attractiveness, right age group and similar background and you have all the tinder for lust-at-first-sight.

Growing friendships

It is, indeed, possible that sexual chemistry will coincide with all the other things you need for love and you'll be happy ever after – but how often? I'm all in favour of great sex but, just because you click sexually, it doesn't mean that you have the ingredients or the ability to form a meaningful, long-term relationship. In fact, short-circuiting the necessarily gentle and lengthy process of cultivating trust, friendship and understanding between two people may cut dead a budding relationship when it might otherwise have flourished. Truly loving someone is not something that can come about overnight; it's a delicate flower that needs the right conditions to blossom. Powerful sexual attraction often grows gradually over time, even when there is nothing beyond simple friendliness to begin with. We've seen this process many times in the agency.

'I can spot that chemistry right away,' they say, 'it's either there or it's not.' Many times a day this refrain echoes around the interview rooms where our clients are explaining to us what they are looking for in a relationship. The consultants try to suppress a sympathetic but, perhaps, ever-so-slightly cynical smile. They know how many members *do* fall in love after unpromising beginnings.

No joy for Jasmine

What happened to Jasmine? Well, we looked at over 40 profiles and photos of men I thought she might be interested to meet. Interestingly, she hardly read them, just fast-flicked through the photos. I know all about photo-flickers – except they're usually men. Jasmine's verdict? 'These are OK for men you'd want just a friendship with', she said. She 'knew' immediately that 'He' wasn't on the agency books. I knew she was unwilling to take a risk and explore possibilities, which is what she would have to do to move forward. Even if she'd wanted to join, I wouldn't have felt it right to invite her. Jasmine was missing out on a potential partner by not employing the Domino Dating approach.

Desirable or essential attributes?

I've mentioned – more than once – the women who come to us with a long list of Perfect Partner requirements without which there can be no chemistry. He *must*, of course, have a sense of humour, and be successful and be happy with himself and his chosen occupation. Shared background, values, outlook and interests all get added in. Needless to say, he *must* be physically attractive and 'taller than me in heels'. Then, there are the extras: a sense of irony was a *must* for a marketing professional the other day; 'has to be fit' is a regular *must*, and 'well travelled – possibly lived abroad' seems to be an important *must* for many of our more cosmopolitan women. We listen patiently and write it all down. Important though all these things are, the main thing that will determine whether or not you fall in love is whether these characteristics are 'musts' or merely 'desirables'. It's rare for a woman to meet a man who has all her 'musts', and if he does and she *likes* him as well, then this is truly amazing – quite apart from good sex, falling in love and wanting to spend the rest of her life with him.

L♡vebyte

" I can't forgive you. Even if I could
   You wouldn't pardon me for seeing through you.
   And yet I cannot cure myself of love
   For what I thought you were before I knew you. **"**
   Wendy Cope, 'Defining the Problem'

Love Myth No. 3 – 'If anything bugs me, then there's no chance he'll be right for me'

So many women believe that, if there is just one thing about a man they don't like at the beginning, whether they call it chemistry, character or something in the looks department, then it'll never work. In the agency, we notice that the women who hold this conviction are less likely to get their man.

We conducted a survey where we asked 200 people *outside* the agency, who said they were in happy, long-term relationships, about what they had thought of their partner when they first met. Was it love at first sight, or was love something that grew on them after a friendship had developed?

When the 'It won't work!' factor does work

In this survey of happy couples, only 32% of the men and 22% of the women said they thought their eventual partner was really special when they first met. The most striking feature to emerge was that, on first sight, 24% of the women and 9% of the men had reservations about their would-be partner. These reservations covered everything from deciding their 'other-to-be' was overweight to finding that they talked too much.

Nevertheless, there was still enough interest for these future couples to pursue a friendship, though not with much vigour to begin with. In spite of these inauspicious starts, they had all become long-term 'items'. Could it really be the case that all these people were compromising their principles and accepting second best? Were they just rationalizing? Were there so few potential mates to choose from that they simply settled for the best on offer? Were they so desperate? How did they decide that someone was, indeed, their future love with all that negative nit-picking flying around? Overweight people can lose weight and talking too much is a sure sign of nerves on a first date, but it can be simply for reasons like this that would-be mates are discarded. I'll leave you to draw your own conclusions. However, if someone fulfils, say, 60% of your wish list, then this is pretty good going and you can decide either to ignore the negatives or negotiate through them.

'Ah!' I can hear you thinking, 'you're trying to persuade me not to be so fussy and just get on with it.' All I suggest you do is to look around your local supermarket next time you are doing the shopping and observe all the couples. Do you notice many that appear to you to be, say, as much as 60% OK with one another? Really look! Honestly, these people who are in relationships haven't settled for the wrong person; they're just prepared to accept differences and work at them. So, give it more time and do the Domino Dating routine before you say 'absolutely not'!

L♡vebyte

❝ Marriage makes two one – but which one? **❞**
Anon

Love Myth No. 4 – 'I'll only be fulfilled when I find him'

In spite of the current popularity of the successful single's self-sufficient lifestyle, the myth that life is only complete when one has found a partner is threaded through every strand of our upbringing, especially if we're female. 'There's less focus without that special person. I don't feel entirely fulfilled, but I think I will be when I find someone to share my life', sighed Annette, an overworked and slightly overwhelming university professor, who'd come to see me about joining the agency. She was the last person I would have expected to be affected by this myth as she had a solid background of gender and political awareness.

Maybe the myth was convenient escapism from what had become a burdensome career. Every weekend, she slogged over some article when a deadline was looming. Weekday evenings were taken up with departmental administration which, with more students to teach than ever before, seemed to have quadrupled over the last few years. In short, she had allowed the career she had passionately embraced when she left university to be transformed into nothing short of a nightmare.

SMART BIOG: **Annette – looking for her missing half**

Annette admitted that her work was interfering with her personal life to a considerable extent. What she couldn't see so easily was that she was also becoming embittered with a tendency to complain – negative attributes for romance seekers. Her daily grind had also eroded her social confidence but, Annette felt, if only she had a happy relationship she'd cope much better with everything. Deep inside, she wanted someone who would make her 'complete' and then – miraculously – the rest of her life would be sorted, too. Wishful thinking and self-deception, I thought, but I felt she deserved some solidarity. I recalled my old job of running an adult-education centre. At the time, I was unable to admit the extent to which I colluded with my own overwork and how badly this affected my personal life.

The agency policy is that every applicant should leave our offices with something positive that will make a difference to their lives – and this isn't necessarily membership. Although I didn't invite Annette to join, we talked with a view, I hoped, to helping her see her situation from another angle. She began to realize that nothing would be achieved by joining the agency until she had resolved various life issues and determined her priorities.

In short, Annette needed to say 'No' more often at work and get out there and have some *fun*. She could start by seeing some upbeat friends. Then, what about going on the shopping spree to end all shopping sprees, with a stylish accomplice, and buy some new frocks – using the money she had just saved by not joining the agency? She could also experiment with some make-up – which she badly needed. Cosmetic counters in department stores often have professionals on hand to give you some free make-up advice, which is useful for getting some new ideas. The hair? Well, Annette had lovely long, thick hair that could benefit from a good cut to bring out the bounce and create more of a frame for her face.

The idea behind the suggestions was not to stick a false, cosmetic image onto someone who preferred to look her 'natural' self. Annette was seriously stuck in a rut and I wanted to nudge her into a position where she could make some choices about how she came across to others. She had 'let herself go' a lot which, I suspected, had contributed to her low self-esteem. With her functional and time-warped clothes, I knew that she would have great difficulty in attracting a man. This is always a sensitive matter to address as it can be so hurtful. I asked, did she think the way she looked really portrayed her character and would it interest the sort of man she wanted to meet? She said she knew it didn't.

Could Annette tackle changes as an Action Plan with all the efficiency she normally mustered for her academic tasks – only, this time, making herself the No. 1 Priority Project? She said 'great', she'd do it and that she'd get in touch in a couple of months to tell me how it was going.

A while later, Annette wrote me a letter thanking me for giving her encouragement. Once she had started the ball rolling and introduced some boundaries and buzz into her life, one thing had led to another and she began dating a colleague at work. It felt as if she was 20 all over again. She was really excited about something else too: she had just received approval for a sabbatical year off work to finish writing a book. And her friends said she looked so well.

Annette's case is typical of many who feel that a relationship is *the* answer to their woes. Great neediness, therefore, will be conveyed to any potential date – and they'll rapidly sprint in the opposite direction. The turnabout for Annette is also an example of the Domino Dating Effect – a little bit of pro-activity and success in one area of one's life can directly and indirectly stimulate all sorts of ripples and changes in other areas. Although we all know that happy relationships do make you feel good all over, they're not an answer to trials and tribulations in other parts of your world.

L♡vebyte

 ❝ I do not like my state of mind:
 I'm bitter, querulous, unkind ...
 I shudder at the thought of men ...
 I'm due to fall in love again. **❞**
 Dorothy Parker, from 'Symphony Recital'

Who are the women who get their man?

Achieving a successful, long-term relationship is not, as simple as just clearing the baggage from the last relationship, being less fussy, giving potential partners more time, or sorting out the rest of your life first. Our clients who find themselves with happy endings to their agency membership, are also more likely to have cultivated an open mind, to have explored more possibilities and to have postponed being judgmental till as late as possible. They didn't make snap decisions about whether there's 'chemistry' or whether they'd found 'the right one' till they had given events time to develop.

However busy you are, there is always room for another friend in your life and you may not realize, at first, which one is likely to become someone special. That's Domino Dating again. I know this sounds exactly like your mother speaking but, funnily enough, she was right.

'Right person, wrong time'

It may be that you've found someone with whom you *could* have the relationship of your life with but one of you isn't ready for it. You need more time to build and define your spaces and boundaries before you can relax enough to let sexual sparks fly.

SMART BIOG: Michele changes her tune

Let me tell you about Michele, a good friend of mine. In my second year of running Drawing Down the Moon, she joined up hoping to find a relationship. Michele dated lots of men and had plenty of fun. When I asked her if she fancied any of them, she said 'No', there was definitely no chemistry and, although they were really interesting people, each one bugged her in a different way. I was flabbergasted as I thought there had been two or three who were definitely her type. A while later, all was explained to me: she'd gone on 'hold' as she'd started to see her old boyfriend again. I realized that perhaps she had never quite finished that old relationship. They spent some months trying to start things up again but without success. Finally, they both agreed it was truly over.

Michele was pretty low. 'When you're feeling a bit stronger,' I suggested, 'come back to the agency and meet some more men.' She retorted something along the lines of, 'I can't face doing it again; the whole "shebang" of first dates and getting to know someone new – it's just not me!' 'In that case,' I said, 'why not phone up Charles or Sam?' These were two of the men she'd been dating through us before – men who, I had thought, might have been really interesting for her. She said she wasn't keen because there was *definitely* no potential chemistry. 'Just see them as friends then, they're really nice and they'll cheer you up,' I insisted. She didn't respond and changed the subject. To cut a long story short, Michele has been married to Charles for some 16 years now and there is plenty of electricity in their relationship!

This sort of scenario crops up often: the right person but the wrong time. No matter how right someone is for you, if you're not ready for a relationship – very probably because you're still carrying over emotional obstacles from the past – then you are less likely to be attracted to someone, at least in a healthy way. If this describes you, make some time to think it through.

Look before you leap

Although you should avoid the Shopping List approach, do collect your wits about you and consider the likelihood of long-term compatibility before you even think of falling in love. I don't suggest you do this in a calculating way – just be aware. This is because, if you have differences in a number of fundamental areas, it is all the more important that you have excellent negotiating skills. Do you and he coincide on what is important to you? Are there many things on which you differ?

Mansearch Workout – Compatibility zones

Do this workout the next time you are even thinking of falling in love. Tick the boxes corresponding to how much you have in common:

	Lots	Fair Amount	Little
Age group	☐	☐	☐
Attractiveness level	☐	☐	☐
Sense of humour	☐	☐	☐
Energy level	☐	☐	☐
Attitudes	☐	☐	☐
Upbringing	☐	☐	☐
Emotional communication	☐	☐	☐
Sex drive	☐	☐	☐
Ambition	☐	☐	☐
Culture	☐	☐	☐
Ethnicity	☐	☐	☐
Music (type)	☐	☐	☐

Current affairs	☐	☐	☐
Politics	☐	☐	☐
Education	☐	☐	☐
Smoking	☐	☐	☐
Drinking	☐	☐	☐
Exercise	☐	☐	☐
Domesticity	☐	☐	☐
Tidiness/untidiness	☐	☐	☐
Type of friends	☐	☐	☐
Lifestyle	☐	☐	☐
Fashion	☐	☐	☐
Leisure interests	☐	☐	☐
Spending habits	☐	☐	☐
Wanting children	☐	☐	☐
Religion	☐	☐	☐
Spirituality	☐	☐	☐

Other things that are important to you:

....

....

Be careful not to be seduced by someone with whom you have only a small number of factors in common unless you know you're good at working out the (highly probable) resulting problems. The fewer the compatibility zones you share, the more important it is to compensate by developing and fine tuning your communication skills so that differences can be accommodated and negotiated with ease.

Are you on his wavelength?

Experts suggest that our dominant thinking and communication style plays a large part in determining our compatibility with another person. If two people already use the same preferred thinking and communication style, they will have fewer disagreements and will be more able to adjust to each other's differences. The more aware you are of someone's thinking style, the easier it is to 'tune in' to it and establish the rapport needed to build and maintain a loving relationship over time. Even if you disagree, you can still establish rapport by communicating in *their* terms. If the person to whom you are attracted shares your thinking style, you are already in prime position to accommodate any differences as you move forward into a loving relationship. However, if this isn't the case, then you will have to work just a bit harder at sorting out differences.

For the next Workout, start by identifying your own preferred thinking style so that you will find it easier to recognize a person who is on your wavelength. This will also help you to realize when you may be unintentionally out of step with a man who attracts you and with whom you want to develop a loving relationship. Of course, this won't necessarily mean love for ever after, but it does mean the signs are more propitious.

Preferred thinking styles are just one helpful signpost for checking out the likelihood of a new relationship moving on into a more meaningful one. Don't, however, give up if your styles are very different; you can learn to tune into each other's patterns by reflecting theirs in the way you communicate. If, for instance, he has a tendency to an auditory style, then use words and phrases relating to sound and hearing and you will be surprised how well it harmonizes the relationship. If he uses lots of visual, or feeling, words and phrases, then match these with similar ones of your own so you are more in tune. It is to this technique that many top communicators owe their success. This Workout is a useful first step in familiarizing yourself with this strategy.

Mansearch Workout – Finding your preferred thinking and communication style

Think of an important happening in your life, something of which you have a clear memory. Try to recreate the memory of this. Do your best to remember the sights, the sounds and the feelings. Describe the event to yourself now and write it down here. What sort of words and phrases are you mainly using – auditory, visual or words about feelings and touch?

Visual words and phrases:

....

....

Auditory words and phrases:

....

....

Feeling words and phrases:

....

....

Now practise observing other people's preferred thinking styles by tackling the next Workout.

Mansearch Workout – Determining other people's thinking and communication styles

♡ Using the knowledge and experience you gained from the previous *Workout,* start listening to conversations between people at work, and amongst your friends. See if you can detect their predominant thinking styles.

♡ Notice what sort of words and phrases they are using – are they mainly auditory, visual or more about feelings and touch.

♡ Once you have spotted the person's preferred thinking style, see if you can match or reflect it in the way you communicate – and then mismatch it by using a different thinking style and note the effect.

♡ Be careful that you don't do anything that looks mocking and might cause offence!

Friends turn into lovers just as lovers turn into friends

What if you are in a 'just friends' relationship and you gradually become aware that you are feeling some real emotional electricity and you want to change gear, become lovers and maybe explore commitment? Giving out unexpected signals that now you fancy him – after, say, five years of friendship – can be confusing and might even scare him off, if this happens too quickly.

Good timing is essential and so is the ability to take a risk in making this leap. However, when you are old, wouldn't you rather regret the things you did try that didn't work than the things you never tried at all?

The important thing is not to jeopardize the friendship by 'coming on too heavy' and scaring him off. Choose a relaxed moment with plenty of time afterwards to allow things to settle. It's a good idea to say something along the lines of, 'I realize that I could feel a lot more for you than just great friendship and that I'd be so happy if we could be lovers. You don't have to say anything now. I'll leave the ball in your court. But, whatever, I don't want to lose you as a special friend.' The main point is not to use any pressure and to leave a genuine option open of just continuing as you are.

SMART BIOG: **Sandy gets closer to Trevor**

Sandy applied for a job with us and told me at the interview how she found her wonderful husband Trevor. He'd been 'just a friend' for eight years and they'd never fancied one another. Then, one day, when they had been shopping for a suit for him to wear at her brother's wedding, he had to leave her for an hour to drop by at his girlfriend's flat. While he was gone, Sandy found herself thinking: 'I don't like this, I really don't like him going to see another woman', and she realized with amazement that she was jealous. On his return, when they were having lunch with her family, Trevor mentioned that his girlfriend thought there was 'something going on' between him and Sandy, and he laughed dismissively. Sandy found herself saying, 'Yes, actually, I-I-I think there could be.' The gobsmacked Trevor's mouth fell open and he dropped a large plate of food on the floor at her feet. They were married eight months later.

Men who are scared of commitment – but not too scared

Even if it did take eight years, Sandy and Trevor were finally ready to fall in love at the same time. Often it's the case, however, that one person is ready and the other isn't yet – but may be in the near future. If you think you might have met your best friend and lover for life, but he needs more time to come to terms with this amazing thought – hold back! Take it easy. Give him some time. This will give him a chance to feel emotionally safe. It's normal for people to be nervous of commitment, especially if a previous relationship has broken down.

Pursuing a man who appears unwilling to commit is always a gamble. How do you know if it's permanent? If his fear is really deep-seated, then no amount of emotional space will make him feel safe. If he is youngish, then there is a good chance he'll grow out of it; but if he's past his early forties and has never been in a committed relationship, don't waste your valuable time. If, on the other hand, he's over 40 and has had committed relationships in the past, then he may just need time to recover – especially if he's just been through a divorce or bereavement.

SMART BIOG: **Lena takes her time**

Lena was a 35-year-old interpreter who'd made about half a dozen good friends with agency men whom she continued seeing for several months on an informal basis – lunch, tennis, a film, a country walk, etc. She did have a couple of flings during that long, hot summer, but she made it clear that that was all they were.

She was much more careful with any of the men she felt could become a serious prospect. When they made romantic advances, she'd ask them to slow down and give her more time. Brian, a 35-year-old architect, was one of them. His longest relationship had lasted 18 months. Yes, there had been many occasions when he wanted to make love to her, but although she fancied him like crazy, she had a strong hunch – from what he had told her about his past – that he would flee once a woman allowed him to get close, emotionally or physically. He was quite a charmer, but Lena's strategy of holding back made the scared part of Brian feel safe and he became very relaxed with her. To his own surprise, for the first time in years he allowed himself to respond to someone. He told me that at first he thought she was playing hard to get and the thrill of the chase spurred him on. Then he realized that, by insisting on maintaining space between them, Lena had helped him learn something important about himself. He got in touch with his feelings and the relationship grew. Lena wasn't sure that he was the one for her until several months had passed and he really opened up. They gave me their story when they both suspended their membership while they went on 'hold'. Lena went first, and it was with baited breath that we waited for a similar request from Brian. It came two months later. The last I heard of them was a card from the Maldives where they had gone for their honeymoon.

Not rushing things, and allowing space for friendship to grow, may be difficult when you're impatient to find your man and time isn't on your side. However, as in Lena's case, you could suspect that an early consummation of the relationship might cause him – or you – to back off fast, having got too close too quickly.

L♡vebyte

" Love: an agreement on the part of two people to overestimate each other. **"**
EM Cioran

Essential and desirable attributes for love

In Chapter 2, I asked you to think about happy couples you know and how they might have modified their original wish lists for a partner. Now I want you to do this for yourself and tackle the next two Workouts. Take your time and think about them. These are good to do with a friend who might, more than once, take you to task over your responses! First, look at the essential qualities you're looking for in a life partner.

Mansearch Workout – Attributes for love (1)

The essential qualities in my life partner would be:

1) ....

2) ....

3) ....

4) ....

5) ....

And any other *essential* qualities:
....
....

Next, note down some of the non-essential qualities you'd like as a bonus. This is where you can say he must be over six-foot tall, have all his hair and, of course, be in touch with his emotions – oh, and no baggage.

Mansearch Workout – Attributes for love (2)

The desirable qualities of my life partner would be:

1) ....

2) ....

3) ....

4) ....

5) ....

And as many more *desirable* qualities as you can think of:

....

....

....

....

Now, and this is the important bit, try stretching your horizons and see how many qualities can be moved from your Essentials list to your Desirables list! Think carefully about this. Remember, relationships are made and not found, and if a potential partner has some 60% of the qualities you desire, then this is pretty good going. Embark on a bit of emotional risk-taking. Again, let me remind you to look at happy couples that you know. How many of them, do you imagine, are with a partner who had *everything* they were looking for? Did they take risks?

Following my own advice?

I would never have had my three wonderful relationships if I'd stuck to the typical Perfect Partner Shopping List that women bring to me when they first come to the agency. Take height – women love to say they want their man to be between 5' 10" and 6' 3" – even if they're petite themselves. Of course, he must be the practical, manly type able to remove spiders from the bath (essential!), and no woman wants a man with 'leftovers' from the past. If he's divorced with children it's a case of 'Next please'.

L♡vebyte

" Oh, life is a glorious cycle of song,
A medley of extemporanea;
And love is a thing that can never go wrong;
And I am Marie of Roumania. **"**
Dorothy Parker, 'Comment'

SMART BIOG: **My own happy ending**

My man number one was a 6' 6" (!) alpha male. He positively towered above me. However, by way of practical, manly skills he was utterly hopeless. I well recall an early date – a first-night performance at London's Royal Opera House after which I found I had a flat tyre. Who changed the wheel? I did, clad in full-length gold lamé and false eyelashes top and bottom – egged on by the cheers of Covent Garden Market porters while my alpha male sat in my car reading an erudite journal. I loved it – and I loved him. We were to have many wonderful years together. We're still best friends and I adore his wife and children.

Man number two was 5' 4½" inches tall – although it wasn't apparent at first sight because of several inches of Afro-style hair on top (it was a long time ago). However, his Irish charm, wit and eccentricity were the great attractions. Our first date was a picnic beside the river Thames during which I thought that he'd had a heart attack, so loud was a sudden scream he emitted. This Irishman was genuinely *terrified* of a tiny mouse that had attacked our baguette and brie, necessitating a rapid departure to a 'safer' spot – much to my amusement! We went on to have several happy, if bumpy, years together and now my husband and I often visit him and his wife in the South of France

Man number three was first spotted, with a worried look on his face, moving a large lawn mower into a fourth floor, gardenless flat next to mine. He was, I discovered, to be my new neighbour. For starters, his 5' 8½" of height was well short of mine when I was perched on my killer heels. I had heard that he was freshly separated and had two young children, now living abroad, so I guessed there would be past-life pitfalls aplenty. I reminded myself that my avowed policy, as a singleton in this type of situation, was to run extremely fast in the opposite direction. However, I couldn't help but be just a *little* curious, so I spied on him that evening through my darkened window. A sight met my eyes that, in those days, would have made most women *very* nervous: he was washing up – OK, that's great, I'll allow – but wearing PINK rubber gloves! Sexy? No way! Love at first sight? Forget it; but yes, you've guessed, we grew to love each other madly and could not now be happier than we are – admittedly after having tiptoed around loads of old problems. Sebastian's passion, romantic spirit, wit, kindness, boyish charm and twinkly green eyes still have me weak at the knees. We've been married for years, but we'd never have got off the starting blocks if I'd stuck to that Perfect Partner List. As for finding a man who remembers to put down the toilet seat every time, forget it girls. But hey, it's a small price to pay for true love.

Keynotes & Diary Prompts

1 Shift from your Essentials to your Desirables Perfect Partner Shopping List as many attributes as possible.
2 Ask a happy couple what, if anything, did they each drop from their Perfect Partner Shopping Lists.
3 Look at good past relationships you've had and ask yourself whether any of the men's qualities were a surprise to you. Does your present Partner Shopping List allow for such surprises?
4 No first-date chemistry – but lots of laughs? Get friendly and you may have found the love of your life.
5 Practise identifying your own and other people's preferred thinking and communication styles by listening to the sort of language they use. Do they most often employ seeing, hearing or feeling words?
6 Practise establishing rapport with people by mirroring their communication style – seeing, hearing or feeling words. Do the same with their body language.
7 Dump any love myths that may be undermining your chances.

RELATIONSHIP ACTION PLAN 9

Note down your Smart Action points for the next week.

Positive Action 1:

....

....

Positive Action 2:

....

....

Positive Action 3:

....

....

Treats

I hope all this reading of *Smart Dating* isn't keeping you stuck indoors. Often, work and life doesn't seem to leave any energy for fun. However, as I hope you're beginning to discover, fun and self-nourishment generate their own energy. So let's get moving!

♡ *Walk somewhere beautiful this weekend* – the gardens of a not-too-far-off stately home, or your nearby hills. It's sometimes very diffi-cult to coordinate suitable times with walking friends. This is where groups such as the Ramblers Association are invaluable. For a very small annual fee, you can go (or not go) on pre-arranged country walks where you can alternate chatting to friendly people with 'musing' on your own. Try a free-sample ramble with your local group.

♡ *Invite yourself to visit some cheerful, positive out-of-town friends,* whom you possibly haven't seen for a while, and rekindle the friendship while enjoying the change of surroundings.

♡ *Organize some free time by setting up an exchange sleep-over for your offspring* (perhaps different-venue sleep-overs, if you've got dozens). Next, arrange a full evening out somewhere exciting (better still, a day and an evening) for yourself.

Although terrified of mice, Emily couldn't help being attracted to rats.

chapter 10

Imperfect Partners

Will he be a prince – or a frog?

There are millions of wonderful men in the world, so why are so many women attracted to the ones who make them unhappy? The particular type we fall for and why is the subject of another book. Suffice to say that we've heard of all of them at the agency.

In their first consultation with us, many women bemoan past foolish choices and show a determination to turn over a new leaf. They know from experience that, unless a man is young-ish, it's rare for him to change his spots. 'It's just a phase he's going through' is a thought that may have comforted them in the early stages of a difficult relationship; but, after a couple of precious years have sailed by, most women are forced to admit that the phase is here to stay.

Choosing the Rat–Men

The list of foolish choices is as long as the list of women seemingly eager to use it. I've mentioned before how often women tell us: 'If there's a Rat-Man in a crowd, I'm sure to find him!' Particular penchants include Elusive-Man, Unavailable-Man, Can't-Commit-Man, Narcissistic-Man, Menopausal Man, Danger-Man, Baby-Phobe-Man, Workaholic-Man, Feelings-Man (only *his* feelings, mind you), Personal-Development-Man, Broody-Man, Peter-Pan-Man ...

It takes two to tango

Remember, though, and this is crucial, it takes two people to make a relationship. These men would not survive in a relationship if their dates or partners had

not colluded with them. In times when women were more economically dependent on men, women had little choice but to be at the beck and call of a partner
who might ignore their needs. Nowadays, however, women – especially those
from the professional strata of Western cultures – can do much to ensure that
they're not trapped in destructive relationships. This does not mean that we are
free of the influence of our social, cultural and psychological conditioning, but
that we're in a stronger position to negotiate problems and to resist being the
victims of our background. The first step is to get to know your own pattern of
relationships. Even if you think there isn't one, and you perhaps see-saw between
opposites, this in itself is a pattern.

'He's the one for me!'

In my experience, many women make a bee-line for a particular type of man.
Even though you may not see many obvious similarities, he's most probably got
something in common with your father (if he was around for you). Even if he's
not like your father in any obvious way, you may still be seeking a similar type
of daughter/dad relationship. If you disliked your father, or looked down on
him, you might, instead, be scouring the earth to find a man who's the opposite. Often, we may even try to resolve unfinished emotional business by seeking, with a father-substitute partner, a 'happy ending' to our unsatisfactory
daughter/dad relationship. These parent-projection issues are as relevant to the
maternal line. If, for instance, you felt sorry for your mother in any way (perhaps for being an underdog), you may find that you're unconsciously seeking
a similar relationship with your partners.

If you went to a mixed-sex school or had, when you were growing up, a brother
or other boys around with whom you felt comfortable, then you're more likely to get along easily with men as friends in the pre-relationship stages. As a
result, you are much less likely to label men as right or wrong for you *before*
you've got to know them and you'll become *friends* with *more men* which is
stacking the odds in your favour – remember the Domino Dating Effect?

The lure of the unsuitable

But why *do* some of us find unsuitable men so exciting? Often it's the aura of
danger or challenge surrounding them that makes them so attractive. Whether
it's the thrill of the chase, the rescue, the frisson of taming the tiger or just
'mission impossible' – it's sexy. Nice, suitable men who are good relationship
material may not present this excitement.

However, the more we become aware of the motives which drive us to take on these dubious challenges, the less power they have over us – hence all the talking therapies. By tackling the Workouts to come, you can begin to get some feedback on why you go for the men you do. You can also take active steps to find 'Relationship-Man' more exciting and sexually attractive.

Early influences that leave their mark

Before beginning to examine the connections between the type of man that attracts you and the patterns of attraction that were programmed in during your early years within the family, ask yourself if these experiences were positive, mixed (that's most of us) or 'doubtful'?

♡ Did you have really good parenting?

♡ Did you respect your mother and your father?

♡ Did they have a fulfilling relationship and were they faithful to one another?

♡ Was your father around?

♡ Did you and he get on well?

If the answer to most of these is 'Yes', then you have a fundamental advantage and are less likely to have relationship difficulties.

L♡vebyte

❝ I sometimes think that God, in creating man, somewhat overestimated his ability. ❞
Oscar Wilde

If you a had problematic relationship with either parent when you were young – or, indeed, if there was the absence of a relationship – then you may pick partners who mirror this less positive side of your upbringing. However, please don't get hung up on analysing your past; it's not always a good predictor of the future. An illuminating glimpse into deep analysis of our psyche comes from the fact that we have plenty of agency members who are psychotherapists themselves and who have presumably examined their relationship patterns minutely. These women are just as likely to insist on choosing men who are the extreme opposite of their past failed partnerships. Often, they are looking for a man so perfect he doesn't exist.

L♡vebyte

❝ The trouble with some women is that they get all excited about nothing – and then marry him. ❞
Cher

Our job as matchmakers is to get you to relax, to have fun and to broaden your horizons. This way, you won't fruitlessly seek the impossible.

SMART BIOG: Margot triumphs

By way of illustration, I'd like to tell you about Margot, a 34-year-old housing-association worker and would-be agency member, who admitted that she was invariably attracted by the very characteristics in a man that later got in the way of a good relationship. As she explained to me when she enquired about the suitability of the agency for her, it was always someone emotionally needy who pressed the 'He's the one for me' button.

Sean, Margot's ex-husband, a director of a series of small businesses, had used her as a crutch. She earned most of their modest income and organized their social life. She spurred him on when his confidence was down – which was often, as business was frequently bad. He filled her need to feel needed – as did her job, where her clients were mostly disadvantaged people.

In the end, Margot had started to feel resentful of, and let down by, Sean's lack of ability to function. When she found herself contemplating temping during one summer holiday, in order to bail him out of his latest financial disaster, she realized she could take no more and left him. They eventually divorced.

That was a couple of years before Margot came to see us. I suspected there might be relationship problems because she seemed emotionally needy. Before enquiring about what she was looking for in a future partner, I asked her to give me a snapshot account of her relationships. What were the worst aspects and the best? The list didn't surprise me. If Margot had tackled the next Workout this is what she might have written:

Mansearch Workout – Example: What Margot said about men she was attracted to

Name of partner	Positive qualities	Negative qualities
Aidan	Playful, funny, sense of humour, handsome, tall	Emotionally needy, bad organizer, disaster prone, expected other people to help him out of scrapes
Gordon	Happy go lucky, entertaining, skilful lover	Bad with money, in debt, wouldn't take grown-up jobs, smoked
Andrew	Romantic image, life and soul of parties, fun	Emotionally stuck, moody, abused alcohol, demanded emotional support
Sean	Optimistic (in bursts), appreciated her support, expressed his feelings, sensitive, good sex	Addicted to dramatic situations. Needed a lot of attention & support, hopeless with money, constantly borrowing

Aidan wasn't mature – yet Margo was initially attracted to his youthful sense of humour and boyish charm. It turned out he needed more of a mother than a partner. Gordon was bad with money – Margot was attracted to his happy-go-lucky attitude to life – but she had to be the anchor.

Andrew, with whom Margot had spent five years, was a dreamer and lived in a fantasy world where music and singing were the exclusive vehicles for his emotional expression. He would never tell her he loved her and yet, she told me, it was his romantic image that had been the initial attraction. Again, she was to fall into the role of being the fulcrum – for their domestic life as well as his musical career. She suspected that he might be on the borderline of having a drinking problem, but felt that her presence had stopped it developing and this was perhaps, she admitted, what kept them together for so long.

Margot had projected an imaginary wish list onto Andrew whereby be could fulfil her yearning for love and her role as a 'rescuer'. In the end, his moodiness and lack of responsibility depressed her so much that, when she was intro-duced to Sean at a party, she was immediately entranced by his upbeat approach to life.

Sean had just started a new business and was in one of his optimistic moods. He seemed to be able to talk about his feelings and acknowledged hers from the start – a rare thing in a man, she thought. She started seeing him regularly and finished the relationship with Andrew. She harboured feelings of guilt about the split but, before long, these were overtaken by the new nursemaid role she allowed herself to be drawn into with Sean whom she soon married. Soon, she began to feel resentful again, and the relationship broke up with much sadness on both sides.

It's not hard to spot the common features in these relationships. The magnetic negatives in the men we fall for usually reflect some elements of our own self, childhood, relationships with parents and even early lovers. Margot volun-teered a bit about her early years. She was an only child with two doting par-ents. Her father's small hardware shop was often on the verge of bankruptcy and her mother would then have to help out. This, alongside of caring for Margot and her own work as an artist, was exhausting and had pushed her mother to the edge of a nervous breakdown. Both parents were constantly res-cuing down-and-out artist friends who sponged off their limited resources. Her father had a couple of affairs when Margot was in her teens – she guessed this because he sometimes called her mother by other women's names. Margot pretended not to notice but felt betrayed on behalf of her mother.

L♡vebyte

❝ A sure sign that a man is going to be unfaithful is if he has a penis. **❞**
Jo Brand

Although Margot's childhood was colourful she, nevertheless, had no role models of really grown-up people who were able to take responsibility for themselves. So although she grew up with a great capacity to love and care, it was often focused on unsuitable men who could not love her back in an equal way. Margot mentioned that she had seen a relationship counsellor for a while. She now understood that she needed to learn to love herself as much as those she cared for before she would attract the sort of men with whom she could develop a mature and balanced relationship.

After hearing Margot's story, I suggested that, before joining the agency, she consider going back to the relationship counsellor to confront and maybe resolve her tendency to fall for men with such negative characteristics. Otherwise, she might continue avoiding men with good relationship potential and hanker after the lure of emotionally needy men. I knew that the formative influences in her life that had led to this behaviour couldn't be undone. However, by coming more aware of them, she could avoid letting them rule her actions – and this is exactly what she did.

After six months of further counselling, Margot came back. She felt she was better able to recognize the danger signals emanating from men needing to be looked after. She registered with us and, to cut a long story short, at the time of writing this book she's 'on hold' with Simon, an energetic deputy head in a secondary school. They dated for five or six months before the relationship took off. 'I'm not sure,' she had uttered (predictably) when I asked her in the early days how things were developing. I guessed rightly, I think, that she still hankered for some of the frisson she knew so well from her earlier relationships before she would allow herself to be attracted to him romantically.

As the result of her counselling sessions, Margot knew she had to tackle things differently. Nudged along by the agency team, she learned to become less dependent on being immediately attracted to a man. Instead, she relaxed and enjoyed cultivating a lively and flirtatious friendship with Simon. Trust and understanding grew and, before long, a healthy emotional chemistry developed that was much more powerful than she had experienced before. I know she won't be the nursemaid in this relationship which appears to be much more egalitarian and balanced.

Cared for and caring

There's a part of all of us that responds to neediness and, in its milder manifestation, it is one of the spices that make life and love so interesting and exciting. Both people in any healthy relationship will, at times, need to be caring as well as cared for – it's a way of expressing their love. Problems arise only when people are totally unaware of their tendency (one way or the other) and allow it to dominate the attraction process. This leads to a one-sided and unhealthy dependency relationship.

How often have you found that a man was wrong for you when you thought he was right in spite of having believed you'd learned from past mistakes? The problem is that we are often completely unaware of why someone attracts us; or, if one part of us understands, there are other parts which refuse to.

It's easy to point a finger at a particular friend and note that they always tend to get into 'difficult' relationships. It's not always as easy to look back on one's own past and perceive dysfunctional patterns of attraction as well as learn from them.

Try out the following Workout yourself. You'll need to find a quiet time when you'll be undisturbed and able to think clearly about what you were drawn to in previous relationships. You should make an honest list of all the things about each person that were both positive and negative. No one is perfect and there is always some kind of trade-off between someone's good and bad sides. Remember, one woman's negative may be another's positive and vice versa. Then, and this is the interesting part, note down under 'Significant Others' any of the qualities in the relationship or person which might be an echo, however, distant, of relationships with parents or early lovers.

Mansearch Workout – Past qualities of attraction

List of qualities in men you've been attracted to:

Partner's name	Positive qualities	Negative qualities	Significant other they might remind you of
1)			
2)			
3)			
4)			
5)			

What patterns emerge? Are your own positive or negative qualities reflected in the men? Do any patterns from your childhood or early relationships spring to mind? These can have an electric effect on sexual attraction. If your positives are mirrored more than your negatives, then there is a better chance of the relationship being a happy one. If there is evidence of a pattern of negativity in the men you choose, where does it come from? Looking back to your earlier life, are there any people or relationships that might have had an influence on your choice of men? Is there a common denominator – something that is likely to get in the way of a healthy relationship developing?

If, each time a relationship goes wrong, you think it's just bad luck – think again. The more aware you are of the danger signals, the easier it is to stop in your tracks and try to tune into the more constructive side of your personality.

L♡vebyte

SMART BIOG: Sonia grows up – and grows away

Here's another example of a bad chooser. Sonia, aged 31, was the intelligent
and exceptionally attractive director of a small, specialist public-relations
company. She was the flip side of Margot. Rather than being attracted to relationships where her partner was always leaning on her, she had been drawn to
men whom she could lean on. They were often quite a bit older and richer or
enjoyed more than average success in their chosen profession.

It's true that these men got a kick out of taking care of Sonia, but how many
of them loved her for who she was rather than as a beautiful accessory to their
successful lives? Initially, Sonia enjoyed basking in this role. Her most recent
and longest-standing boyfriend had been Richard, who was 48, divorced and a
partner in a leading firm of commercial solicitors. When they had first met,
Sonia was only 26 and very happy to be wined and dined at the best restaurants, taken on lovely holidays and be generally cosseted.

The fact that she didn't take responsibility for very much in the relationship
was something that bothered neither of them in the first couple of years. But
then, as Sonia grew older and more mature, she started to want greater independence and began to voice her opinions more assertively. Her work was
going well and she became more of her own person and took on an increased
proportion of the decisions in their relationship. Richard, however, who had
never been close to a woman as his equal, began to feel uncomfortable – and
jealous of her whenever she wasn't with him.

L♡vebyte

" By the time you swear you're his,
Shivering and sighing,
And he vows his passion is
Infinite, undying –
Lady make a note of this:
One of you is lying. "
Dorothy Parker, 'Unfortunate Coincidence'

While Sonia was growing out of her dependence on Richard, he, more than ever, needed to be the carer and the father figure – and this was unlikely to change. The upshot was that Richard, not wanting to be the one who was dumped, left Sonia and almost immediately found someone else to take under his wing – at least for a while. Sonia wasn't even terribly upset over the split. She felt that her experience with Richard had been part of her growing up and she was now ready for something quite different.

She joined the agency and gained even more confidence in her new-found self by making a lot of friends amongst the men to whom she'd been introduced as potential partners. At the time of writing, Sonia has had a couple of flings and has just gone on hold with Peter, a doctor, who is her age and shares her passion for sub-aqua. He is a lovely man and he wants to settle down with an independent woman who knows what she wants. Above all, he respects her.

In Sonia's case, her over-dependency was something she grew out of as she become more mature and confident. Nevertheless, a particular need often continues to dominate relationships. This usually has to be confronted if it is not to undermine happiness.

L♡vebyte

" A pessimist is one who, when he has a choice of two evils, chooses both. "
Oscar Wilde

In all good relationships, each person's dependence and independence needs can be met; but, when the balance is all one way, it can lead to tears. This is especially likely if one of the partners is much younger. When that person grows up and matures, they often leave behind their need to be dependent. The older partner then becomes redundant. The pages of celebrity gossip magazines are littered with the refugees from such relationships. The same thing is likely to happen if there is any kind of imbalance of power that can affect a change of roles: in such a case the relationship needs to be strong to survive.

How often have you wasted a lot of time 'just waiting' for an unsuitable partner to change into the person you think you want? If you're both young, then there is more likelihood of change, but older people rarely shift their base line. You may need to face up to this. It can be painful. Much better to be able to identify the losers early on – but how? What are the secrets?

Spotting the losers

Yes, you can spot the losers. The tendency is to repeat the past – it's a script we know well. However, you may go to the opposite extreme, thus denying yourself realistic options in the middle. Apart from all the danger signals that you are now well aware of since the last workout, common sense should also set alarm bells ringing. If past relationships have always gone wrong, think twice if you encounter any of the following:

You desperately fancy him	Chances are he's pressing that 'He's the one for me' button that was programmed in by previous dysfunctional encounters and/or early family relationships. Wait till you've been going out for a while before you have sex or make any kind of commitment statements. You need more time to know where you really stand before becoming involved.
He looks like the guy you just split up with	Yes, you may be still hankering after writing a happy ending to the script of your last bad relationship.

Your friends say – 'There you go again.'	They can spot it – you resist doing so.
You say to your friends – 'There's no chemistry – he could be an *extremely* good friend, but I'm not looking for that so I won't see him again.'	In other words he *cares* for you. In your previous relationships you went for men who treated you badly and you accepted it, which indicates low self-esteem.
You're always apologizing for his behaviour to your friends and family	You know he's not right for you. You can't change his behaviour – only he can do that.
You feel you could 'help him' or 'reform him'	Hot danger signals. You've been there, you've done this before. What's going on? Stop and think.
You feel extremely insecure in your new relationship	A certain amount of wobbly knees is inevitable, but if it's the deep-down fear of hurt and loss, and the relationship is still in the early stages, then consider whether you are carbon-copying the past. Talk to a counsellor, or at least to your closest friends, about your feelings.
He puts you on a pedestal and insists you stay there	He's projected a fantasy onto you. The real you may not be what he wants.
He's never been in a long-term relationship and he's over 35	Is he scared of emotional closeness?
He loves someone else	Mission almost impossible. Are you seeking rejection?
He's way above your class attractiveness-wise	Are you homing in on rejection yet again?
He's verbally or physically abusive	Does this reflect some aspect of your childhood?

He demonstrates serious addictive or obsessional habits	Are you seeking out someone likely to hurt you?
He lives really far away	Long distance love is **very** difficult, indeed. Another mission almost impossible. Are you nervous of intimacy?

'How do I attract decent men'

Now that you know both your particular attraction pattern and what makes you miserable in a relationship, you can decide to choose only men who treat you well and make you happy. Easier said than done?

To help you in your mission, you can again employ the potent technique that I outline for you in Chapter 8 and which is adapted from NLP (Neuro-Linguistic Programming). This powerful tool is used by top communicators, world leaders and all kinds of people who seek to modify their reactions and behaviour. Here's how to use it in this context.

After you've completed the previous Workout and seen where your attraction patterns might stem from in your life, find a quiet moment with a pen and some paper. Try to visualize the person you are looking forward to being: a person who has left the past behind her and is happy in a relationship. Start by remembering how you felt when you were in a previous relationship that was working well. Alternatively, you could use a friend who is in a good relationship as a role model – or else you can just 'imagine'. Write down the characteristics that inspire you. Here are some suggestions:

♡ They think well of themselves.

♡ They expect others to think well of them.

♡ They respect their own as well as their partner's needs.

♡ They expect their man to respect others' needs as well as his own.

♡ They are assertive (not aggressive) in communicating needs and wants clearly and directly, but with sensitivity.

♡ They stand up for themselves.

♡ They are clear about the boundaries between acceptable and unacceptable behaviour from their man.

♡ They make clear requests for change in unacceptable behaviour. If, after this, it continues they will finish the relationship.

♡ They are attractive.

Having made your list of the personal characteristics of someone in a good relationship, the next step is to visualize that person as you. Try and imagine how you see, hear, feel and use body language in this happy situation. Think of it as a film and put yourself in the central role – and you're playing it NOW. Take the above list as your script and repeat it in the first person. Magnify and sharpen the image of yourself. Intensify the colours, raise the volume, speed up the pace and feel the feelings. You are the star!

Now you are ready to use the powerful technique of 'anchoring' your vision and its accompanying sensations and feelings by associating it with a physical trigger – as you did when creating your **Golden Glow** when we were practising flirting and attraction (see page 161). But this time perhaps your trigger might be to press your ear lobe between your thumb and forefinger while you think of yourself as starring in your film about the New You who makes happy relationships. Practise creating an association between this physical trigger and your positive thoughts. This is the 'anchor' that you can use to trigger your new self into being. What you have to do is to 'fire' your trigger and see yourself starring in your successful-relationship role. Hear the good things you hear from others. Feel the feelings you experience.

Every morning before you go out, practise triggering this New You. Imagine you are the person in your film script: the one whom others treat well and who has high self-esteem. Attractive, interesting and caring men are attracted to you, and you to them. Continue to trigger the image as you go through your day, and each time really tune into, see and feel the accompanying enjoyable experiences. The idea is to 'pretend' until you are this new being – you in a happy functioning relationship. At first this will require determination and may seem odd but don't give up. You can change and stay with this new more positive you.

Notice how people react differently to you. Watch their body language for signals. If anyone comments, explain that you are trying a different tack now and you intend to stick to it. Guess what? After a while the new you will become automatic, and your vision of yourself will be more positive. Your really will be the person you've decided to be. Other people will treat you with more respect. Men who treat women badly won't be making a bee-line for you – nor you them. You will become more attractive to men who care.

'But I really don't fancy decent men'

'Ah' I can hear you saying 'but what if I still don't fancy Mr Nice-Guy sexually?' Give it time. A new mode of relating to men will need a chance to develop. Write an affirmation: '*I will practise Domino Dating and give every man who is "decent, interesting or just a kind friend" the chance to get to know me bet-ter and see if sexual attraction springs up later on – as it does in so many happy relationships for other people*'. The fact that this has never happened for you before doesn't mean it can't happen in the future! Read this affirma-tion every morning and organize your social life around it.

Flirt against your 'man type'

Maybe you never flirt with decent men? If you don't flirt, then they won't pick up on and reciprocate sexual signals – and you won't find them sexually attractive. We tend to fancy men who resemble the ones we've fancied before, and only to flirt with this type. Turn on your flirt signals with decent Relationship-Man, instead of Treat-You-Like-a-Doormat-Man, and you could well find your heart's all a-flutter!

Domino Dating gives you the chance to practise

The Domino Dating Strategy suggests that if you are prepared to date more men – anyone who's 'roughly right' – you will get more practice which will set up a ripple effect and create more confidence and skill in handling dating sit-uations. To increase your success rate, you must expect to increase your failure rate, too. You need to meet more frogs if you are to meet more princes! If you create more dating opportunities, whatever your chosen method, you will have plenty of chances to engage in flirting with Relationship-Man, *and you can thus challenge and change the type of man you've found attractive in the* past. If you're only meeting one single available man every five years, then too bad if he doesn't turn out to be good for you – he's all that's on offer. Go for volume, on the other hand, and you give yourself plenty of choice.

'But I still fancy Rat-Man'

'What if Rat-Man turns up and I just want to rip his clothes off?' No one said this would be easy. The new 'I'm worth it' code is: don't have sex with a man until you know he will respect you. Making love, especially for women, can have a bonding effect that is difficult to ignore. If you sleep with Rat-Man out of pure lust, you will be back in your old addictive pattern of dysfunctional relating.

Meet your own needs

When you are exploring a new relationship, focus on satisfying your own needs as well as your man's. Remember, you are a 21st-century woman with her own life! Don't let your happiness depend solely on one other person, however strongly you feel about them. Cultivate other friends and activities. Enjoy your career and strive to excel at what you do every day. Be your own person.

Might it be just a Rat-Man phase?

There's no easy answer to this one. If he's young, he may mature out of a problematic tendency. A man may also recover in reasonable time if he's behaving badly because he's on a serious rebound from a broken relationship. If he's shown great awareness of a problem and is working on it – maybe with a counsellor or therapist – then it may well be worth hanging on in there for a bit, but don't hold your breath. Keep other options open – always.

Remember, you can't change a man. He can only change himself. Don't waste your valuable time on someone who's a 'no hoper' for you.

Keynotes & Diary Prompts

1 Using your response to the Workout on the positive and negative qualities of your exes, copy out their negative qualities and who they remind you of in your past. Write out an affirmation promising to avoid men who display these qualities in the future.
2 Make a list of the positive qualities of your exes and who they remind you of from your past. Write out an affirmation to ensure that any future men you link up with will have at least some of these qualities, say 60% of them.
3 Work hard on your self-esteem. Be aware that it's important to boost this so that you attract people who mirror your positive qualities in friendships

as well as relationships. Practise 'triggering' this new 'high esteem' inner-you any time you can.

4 Don't collude with your negative qualities. Avoid new, close relationships with men who reflect these qualities.

5 Don't have sex or get deeply involved with a new boyfriend before you've really got to know him and assessed whether he fits your positive or negative relationship pattern. Only go ahead if he fits the positive one.

RELATIONSHIP ACTION PLAN 10

Note down your Smart Action points for the next week.

Positive Action 1:

....

....

Positive Action 2:

....

....

Positive Action 3:

....

....

Treats

TREAT yourself to some luxurious necessities and a few things that might be more unusual for you, before rushing on to Chapter 11!

♡ How about *a hair re-think*? Make sure it's *your* re-think, and not just your hairdresser's. Remember, too, that the main function of your hair at the moment is as a powerful Dating Accessory. Check back to Chapter 8 for what does, and what doesn't, hair-wise, turn men on.

♡ Ring a friend and ask him/her to *arrange a surprise evening or weekend outing* of their choice, and not to give you any details beforehand (except whether you'll need a passport, a G-string or a pair of wellingtons). You can arrange a return outing in the near future.

♡ *Feng Shui your home* – starting with the bedroom. Get hold of a book on the subject and explore the main principles. One of these (which doesn't even need a book) is 'Chuck out everything that doesn't serve a functional or decorative purpose.' If you're stifling the energy of your home with junk, then there's no room for anything new. Look carefully at the relationship corners in all of your rooms (*and* throw some more clothes out of the wardrobe).

Gemma knew her rawlplugs from her grommets, but she found a second opinion never hurt ...

chapter 11

Making it Happen!

Congratulations! You're ready for action. You've practised spiriting yourself into **Dating Mode** – that exciting, anticipatory and flirty state that gets you revved up to get out there and meet fascinating new people. You've taken a look at those **Relationship Blockers** from your past that need ditching – or at least ongoing surveillance. You've checked out, and thoroughly eliminated, any **presentation** and **style** no-nos. You are walking tall and you know that you look and feel a million dollars.

Above all, you're happy in your work and play – by being that **best friend and lover to yourself**, before anyone else. All the tips and strategies in this book will be to no avail if you can't become a contented and happy individual. There is no point in *doing* all the right things if you *feel* wrong, if you're not in the right emotional state to take advantage of the wonderful dating opportunities that I hope you're now longing to create.

To maximize your dating potential, you are now regularly using – and benefiting enormously from – the positive suggestions at the end of each chapter: the **Keynotes & Diary Prompts**, your **Relationship Action Plans** and, above all, the **TREATS**. Make each day an adventure where you try something different, where you explore new possibilities for greater happiness and fulfilment. You will then be ready to embrace that contented and fulfilled relationship with someone wonderful.

To enhance the feel-good factor, surround yourself with people who boost your feelings of self esteem and positivity, whether at work, at play or in your personal life. What do you do with the others – the moaners and groaners? Decide whether you want to a) help them into a more positive space, b) accept them but see them less, or c) dump them. The choice is yours.

I'm not, by the way, suggesting that anyone should spend their entire life spaced out on feel-good hormones; just check that you're getting as much as you need to put you in Dating Mode whenever you want to be ready for that great date and whatever follows.

But ... What's that? ... you still haven't quite got a 'next' date, let alone a 'great date' in the picture! Well, what are you waiting for? *If* you want a life partner, a best friend and lover, what's your plan? Knowing all the theory backwards isn't enough to net you your man – *try* some of the ideas in *Smart Dating* and get out there on some practice dates. A few moments of apprehension could be exchanged for a lifetime of bliss.

In case you're having a mega-attack of cold feet (because you still believe finding a partner should 'happen naturally' without any special effort on your part), here, for good measure, is one last Workout. *Do this even if you haven't done any of the previous ones.*

Mansearch Workout – The ultimate find-a-partner task list

Ask yourself the following questions:

- ♡ How many new men do I plan to meet in the next six months?
- ♡ How I intend to make this happen?
- ♡ What am I going to do today to make this happen?
- ♡ What else will I have done by the end of the next week to make this happen?
- ♡ What more things will I have done by the end of this month to make this happen?

Now write the tasks and dates you have given yourself in your diary – and stick them on the fridge!

Watch points

You've found a possible man, you have a feeling he could be the one, but your friends say, 'Oops, you're at it again!' – meaning you're sabotaging a good opportunity or are about to tread on one of your regular relationship land-mines. Wait! Don't let it happen. Check the Workouts in Chapters 9 and 10 *and try something or someone different.*

Don't let the occasional 'odd ball' blow you off course. When, for instance, you're secretly counting the minutes till you can escape from that first (and last) date – remember **Domino Dating**? To increase your dating success rate, you must, inevitably, increase your failure rate and – let's face it – you can chat to *anyone* for an hour. You won't be embarrassed by leaving promptly as you will have explained beforehand that you have to go early to see your sick Aunty Ethel (or meet that midnight copy deadline or feed the gerbil.)

Set in place your 'I'm fed up with dating' pick-me-up list for implementation after an unexpected run of train-spotters, as there is no guarantee that this can be totally avoided. Your list might include several end-of-the-chapter **TREATS**, from just ringing a cheerful friend to fixing a weekend away (on the other hand, painting the kitchen might do equally well).

What, though, about that painful rejection and the agonizing post-mortem? Think creatively. If one route to a great relationship doesn't bear fruit, don't think 'failure', think 'incredibly useful feedback'. Contemplate what you've learned – and then try something new. There are plenty of terrific men out there, but they mostly get snapped up by those women who are prepared to hunt proactively and capitalize on all opportunities.

If you meet a new man every month for the next twelve months and make good friends with, say, four of them – then there is a good chance of one working out. If not, your girlfriends will be delighted at your generosity in introducing them to some interesting men. With all your new get-up-and-go, and a year ahead that's filled with all sorts of exciting new events (not only of a romantic nature) – you can't help but enjoy yourself!

So, here's wishing you lashings of fantastic fun, frolics and flirtatiousness on the way to meeting that very special someone. Good luck!

Mary

Some Really Inspired Further Reading

Here are some 'must read' titles for anyone eager to brush up on communication skills for finding and keeping a loving partner.

Why We Love: the Nature and Chemistry of Romantic Love by Helen Fisher (Henry Holt and Company, 2005)

Why We Pick the Mates We Do By Anne Teachworth (The Gestalt Institute Press, 2007)

Superflirt by Tracey Cox (Dorling Kindersley 2003)

Teach Yourself Flirting by Sam van Rood (Teach Yourself Books)

Be Your Own Life Coach by Fiona Harrold (Hodder and Stoughton, 2000)

Body Language – How to Read Others' Thoughts by Their Gestures by Allan Pease (Sheldon Press, 1997)

The Flirt Coach by Peta Heskell (Thorsons, 2001)

Hot Relationships – how to have one by Tracey Cox (Corgi, 2000)

How to be a People Magnet – Proven Ways to Polish Your People Skills by Leil Lowndes (Thorsons, 2001)

How to Talk to Anyone by Leil Lowndes (Thorsons, 1999)

Mars and Venus on a Date – 5 Steps to Success in Love and Romance by John Gray (Vermilion, 1997)

The NLP Coach by Ian McDermott and Wendy Jago (Piatkus, 2002)

NLP & Relationships by Robin Prior and Joseph O'Connor (Thorsons, 2000)

Why Men Don't Listen and Women Can't Read Maps by Allan and Barbara Pease (Orion Books, 2001)

A Woman in Your Own Right – Assertiveness and You by Anne Dickson (Quartet Books, 2002)

The Mirror Within: a New Look at Sexuality by Anne Dickson (Quartet, 1995)

The Art of Happiness: a Handbook for Living by HH Dalai Lama and Howard C. Cutler (Coronet Books 1998)

The Transformation of Intimacy: Sexuality, Love and Eroticism in Modern Societies by Anthony Giddens (Polity Press, 1992)

Self-Made Man: My YearDisguised as a Man by Norah Vincent (Atlantic Books 2006)

Want to learn more about my strategies for dating success?

Mary

Check out these forthcoming
dating events and products on:

www.DrawingDownTheMoon.co.uk
or email: **info@DrawingDownTheMoon.co.uk**

Phone: +44 20 793 76263

♡ DVDs, CDs and downloads on various aspects of dating and flirting including interviews with other dating gurus

♡ Smart Dating teleclasses where up to 100 callers participate in a talk on specific aspects of dating

♡ Smart Dating Seminars where singles can hear Mary talk about her secrets of dating success and mix'n'mingle afterwards over a glass of wine

♡ One-to-one date coaching

♡ A talk on successful dating strategies for your club or networking group

Lightning Source UK Ltd.
Milton Keynes UK
UKOW03f0946121213

222887UK00002B/2/P